MAUREEN COULD NOT SLEEP. FIRST SHE TRIED LYING ON HER BACK BUT IT WAS NO GOOD.

Then she tried her side, facing away from Joe, and saw from the alarm clock that it was 11.45. It was still Thursday. She turned again but still could not get comfortable. Perhaps if she had something to eat . . .

Very quietly, so as not to disturb Joe, Maureen eased herself out of bed (the springs creaked) and tiptoed across the bedroom. She padded downstairs and went into the kitchen, turning on the light as she did so. She took the lid off the swing-top bin and peered inside. In fact there was only some damp kitchen towel on top of the piece of cake; the tea-bag had missed it. Perhaps there was some ash on the side.

She picked the cake out of the bin, gave it a quick scrape and ate it, just as Friday began.

SHERRY ASHWORTH

A MATTER OF FAT

A SIGNET BOOK

SIGNET

Published by the Penguin Group
Penguin Books Ltd, 27 Wrights Lane, London w8 5tz, England
Penguin Books USA Inc., 375 Hudson Street, New York, New York 10014, USA
Penguin Books Australia Ltd, Ringwood, Victoria, Australia
Penguin Books Canada Ltd, 10 Alcorn Avenue, Toronto, Ontario, Canada m4v 3b2
Penguin Books (NZ) Ltd, 182–190 Wairau Road, Auckland 10, New Zealand
Penguin Books Ltd, Registered Offices: Harmondsworth, Middlesex, England

First published in Great Britain by Commonword Ltd 1991
Published in Signet 1993
1 3 5 7 9 10 8 6 4 2

Typeset by Datix International Limited, Bungay, Suffolk
Set in 10/13 pt Monophoto Plantin
Printed in England by Clays Ltd, St Ives plc

Thanks to Gill and Colette, for their support
while I was writing this; to my parents and Rona,
for their belief in me; to Robyn and Rachel,
for being there.

This novel is for Brian.

CHAPTER ONE

Helen felt around the inside of the washing-machine to check that no stray sock was left at the back. She shut the glass-fronted door, picked up the basket of washing, and took it into the garden. Katy marched up with an air of importance.

'Can I pass the washing to you, Mummy?'

'Yes, darling. I'll put the basket on the bench so you can reach it.'

One pair of boy's pants, age five to seven. A wait. One grey sock. Another wait. One pink sock. A longer wait. Helen stood forlornly at the washing-line. It was Wednesday the third of October. Katy didn't go to play group on a Wednesday, so she was at home all day. A cotton T-shirt. Helen wondered what they could both do. There was always Heyside Park, of course. Then, with her spirits rising, she considered the possibility of lunch at BurgerBar. Another grey sock. She felt a pang of hunger just thinking about a Burger Supreme. Katy would like it too. Knickers. Then Tony would be late home tonight as he had a job over in Altrincham. So it wasn't worth cooking the chicken. A white vest with the hem coming undone. She'd leave it in the freezer, give the kids fish fingers and beans, and she'd just make do. A boy's track-suit bottoms.

'Waaah!'

'Katy! What's wrong?'

'I felled over.'

'Here. Let me see.'

Helen swung her three-year-old daughter on to her lap and surveyed the damage. Two lightly grazed knees. She kissed them better and remembered that *Playbus* was about to start on BBC1. She carried Katy into the lounge, picked up the remote-control panel from the carpet and activated the set. The child's eyes assumed the familiar expectant look of the well-qualified infant viewer.

And here I am, thought Helen, the world's greatest living expert on children's television. What I don't know about *Postman Pat*! There was a sharp knock at the door. With a tremor of anticipation Helen went into the small hall, and saw through the frosted glass door the broken-up outline of Judith, her next-door neighbour.

'Judith! Why aren't you at work?'

'Period pains. And I've run out of Anadin.'

'Come in. I've got some in the kitchen. Can you have some coffee? Katy's watching *Playbus*.'

'Well, all right. Just a quick one. With skimmed milk.'

Judith perched on the edge of the chair in the dining-room that led through an archway to the lounge. Her dark auburn hair was resplendent with its long shaggy perm. Her carefully made-up eyes looked tired; clearly the period pains were real enough. She wore a low-cut black T-shirt with a wide elasticated black belt that minimized her small waist. A tight black skirt hugged her hips. Helen looked on with admiration, disapproval and envy.

'Would you like a Chocolate Hob-nob?'

'Oh, no!'

'Well, you won't mind if I do.'

'No. Go ahead. It doesn't bother me.'

It wouldn't bother me if I was your size, thought Helen. No, I mustn't feel jealous.

'So, Judith, how's the slimming?'

'Fantastic. I reckon I'll score Bull's-eye tomorrow.'

'I'm not talking about the ladies' darts team, Jude.'

'No, silly. She's set me a Bull's-eye weight of eight seven. That's what I've got to reach. And last week I was eight eight and expecting my period. Well, you always put weight on then. I've been as good as gold this week.'

'How much have you lost now?'

'Three and a quarter stone . . .'

Over the past year Helen had watched Judith's progress from frump to *femme fatale*. It was better than a soap opera. With each few pounds discarded Judith changed perceptibly. Gone were the flowery elasticated skirts and baggy blouses. With the careful circumspection of an MI5 agent Judith sneaked in parcels from Chelsea Girl and Dorothy Perkins when her husband was otherwise engaged. Her pale undistinguished face was transformed by Mary Quant and Max Factor; Heyside Health Club's sun-bed browned her slender limbs. Helen remembered seeing a horror film once, *Dorian Gray*, was it, where this evil man kept the fresh innocent face of his youth while his portrait in the attic grew ugly with his sins. Helen always imagined a fat Judith in a tent-like smock up in her attic, while this artificial sex goddess paraded around downstairs. Certainly you had to admire her.

'Come with me tomorrow, Helen.'

'With you? Where?'

'To Slim-Plicity. My slimming club. I won't be leaving even if I do score Bull's-eye as you've got to maintain your new weight for eight weeks.'

'Oh, no! I couldn't stand the thought of being weighed in front of all those other women.'

'But it's not like that. It's quite private. It would do you the world of good. You don't often go out of an evening.'

'Look. I'll think about it. I don't know.'

'I'll knock tomorrow night. Must be off. If I have a lie down now I might be fit for the office in the afternoon.'

Yes, it was definitely going to be BurgerBar for lunch today!

'Mummy, Mummy, I want to sit on a mushroom!'

Helen placed the grey cardboard tray of food on to the table while Katy bounced on to a children's toadstool brightly painted in red and white. Three of these surrounded a garish green table with a cream base. Helen thought she had better sit with Katy. Where did children eat before we had BurgerBar? Helen couldn't remember. Her daughter nibbled at her burger, allowing the bottom of the bun to hang loose at the back. Helen stirred her coffee with the white sliver of plastic provided. The coffee was too hot to drink. Should she have a Burger Supreme after all? She went back to the food queue and bought herself a Burger Supreme and regular fries. She ate them quickly, without really tasting the food at all. Katy was only half-way through

4

her burger. Helen hoped she would leave some. Meanwhile, Helen looked around her.

Why was it that, despite the pastel décor, the profusion of cheese plants and other greenery, the tasteful paintings and the carefully arranged honeycomb of seats obscuring the sight of other greedy people, BurgerBar failed to convince grown-ups that it was pleasant to eat there? Was it because every BurgerBar, everywhere you went, was exactly the same? Or was it the contrast between the working-class clientele and the décor, or the contrast between the décor and the surrounding shops; Ali's Tandoori Restaurant, Davy's Dry Cleaning, M & R Supa Saver 50p Discount Store? Inoffensive muzak played relentlessly in the background.

A waitress walked around the restaurant putting BurgerBar paper baseball caps on all the children. Katy took hers off immediately.

'Mummy. I don't want my chips any more.'

'Well, never mind. I'll finish them for you.'

'Thank you, Mummy.'

Katy began on her milkshake and Helen thought about an apple pie. She wouldn't be having a proper meal tonight so she might as well. She returned to the food queue.

The hot, juicy filling of the apple pie was inexplicably comforting. Helen wished she could go on eating it for ever. Everything, the people in the restaurant, the shops outside, her own daughter, seemed to slip away into the background and the reality was this sweet, tangy, hot apple pie. Nothing else mattered. It didn't matter, for example, that her stomach was straining against her trousers. Or that Tony wouldn't be home till after nine. Or that it was all so bloody monotonous.

Helen Greenwood was twenty-nine. Brought up in east Manchester, she'd gone to a local comprehensive, and fitted in well. Easy-going, she'd had plenty of friends and lots of opportunities to enjoy herself. She'd liked English, and Mr Stevenson, her English teacher, was always surprised and delighted by the amount that she read. But when he set her an essay entitled 'Why I am Different from My Friends' she could find nothing to say. In Helen's circle it was respectable to be a hairdresser, a secretary or to work with children. Helen got five O-levels, including English Literature, and took a NNEB at the local tech. Her social life became better still.

Her first job was as a nanny to a family in Sale, a very desirable area in south Manchester. The two little boys she cared for were sweet, but there was too much housework and, worst of all, Helen missed conversation and the outside world. She knew nannying was not for her and so she landed a job as a nursery nurse in a private nursery. The wages were appalling, but she supplemented them with some child-minding after hours. It was much more fun working with other girls of her own age, and they did have a laugh. One day Sue at the nursery came in with some brochures about work opportunities in Canada and Helen was tempted. She had all the right qualifications and she'd always wanted to travel. But it was just around this time that she started going with Tony seriously. She'd known him as part of her crowd for ages – he'd studied at the tech with her – but it was different lately.

And sure enough a year later Helen and Tony were married. He'd just established his own business – he was a self-employed computer breakdown engineer. The babies came quickly; they were only married a year when Matthew was born. Katy arrived two years later. Helen couldn't be bothered to return to nursery work after having taken five years off to care for her own two kids, and she was lucky enough to get some part-time work in Sue's husband's sandwich bar in the city. It provided a bit of extra cash and some longed-for social contact. But she was bored. The children were lovely but they weren't exactly stimulating. And what had she achieved in her life? Well, the children, but apart from the children? Maggie, who she used to go to school with, had a university degree, and she wasn't much cleverer than Helen. And what happened to all that reading she used to do? These days it was just magazines.

Helen was bored. Happy, but bored. And it was uncomfortable to admit to this boredom because it begged the question, what are you going to do about it? So real life slipped into the background, and in the foreground there was always food. Crumbly rich chocolate biscuits, large slabs of shortbread, the slow unfolding of boiled sweets, the irritable munching of crisps, shared Chinese take-aways with Tony . . . and lunch in BurgerBar with the kids.

'Are you sure you don't want any more milkshake, Katy?'

'I got a tummy ache.'

Helen pulled the milkshake towards her and sucked at the mud-like grey sludge at the bottom. It was thick and sweet. She put it down, and saw how the contents stayed in the straw, clogging it up. Her gullet felt like that, thought Helen. Her stomach was so full that it felt as if the food, this milkshake, was queuing up in her alimentary canal waiting to get in. She felt an overwhelming revulsion. What was she doing to herself? She was a pig. Her long wavy hair, her baggy T-shirts and jeans hid nothing. She was fat, and she'd better face up to it.

By eight o'clock that evening her resolve had not weakened.

'Tony, are you working late tomorrow night?' Helen inquired of her husband.

'No. I should be home by six at the latest. Any reason?'

'I'd like you to mind the kids. I'm going out with Judith.'

A family pack of Golden Wonder Cheese and Onion crisps. Two packets of dry roasted peanuts. A Mars bar. A half-pound slab of Galaxy. Toffee fudge ice-cream in the freezer. And Joe would probably bring chips back when he got in from the pub. Maureen looked set for a good evening. That was the best part of starting Slim-Plicity again – the night before. The more she ate, the more she'd lose in the first week. She eyed her stock of food affectionately, with mounting excitement.

Now it was a matter of getting the atmosphere right. She took the phone off the hook. She surveyed the paper to see what was on the box. Lovely! *Clarissa* – a rags-to-riches story set in the eighteenth century. On the glass coffee-table her companions for the evening beckoned enticingly. Maureen wondered where to begin. Her mouth watered. She picked up the Golden Wonders and pulled the bag apart with ease, revealing a profusion of naked, golden crisps. She took just one and allowed the flavour to travel the length of her tongue. Another. And another. Two. Three. Better hurry up.

After finishing the crisps and peanuts (washed down with a can of lager from the fridge), Maureen had a twinge of guilt. So she went over to the sideboard and got out her Slim-Plicity card from last time. She read it over. In 1977 she'd lost nineteen pounds. Then she'd put two stone on. She'd lost another stone in 1978, and put it back on in 1979. 1980, two off, one on. She made a rapid calculation. Yes! She now weighed around fourteen stone and since she'd been going to Slim-Plicity she'd actually lost a total of fifteen stone – more than her body weight now. Well, that was encouraging. Maybe this time she'd score Bull's-eye. And so tonight she'd have a good time. She started on the Mars bar.

Maureen loosened her belt. She felt contented. She'd left some ice-cream for Joe too. Just at the moment that she turned off the television she heard the gate open and her husband walk up the garden path. He'd have the key with him, so Maureen resumed her place in the armchair and waited.

'Here, get some plates, love. I've been down the chippy.'

'That's nice. I could just do with some chips.'

'And I've got you a couple of cans of Guinness to wash it down with.'

'You are a love.'

Maureen took her belt off. Despite her large stomach, her impressive midriff and an imposing bosom, she was engaging in appearance. Her naturally curly hair was coloured with reddish tints; her persistence in wearing blue cream eye-shadow showed a strength of character, a desire to look good and a blatant disregard of fashion. She wore blusher that she called rouge. Her generously cut striped dress was sleeveless although it was autumn, as Maureen Evans was prone to hot flushes. It was a disaster when these struck at work, because the school kitchen was an inferno at the best of times. But Maureen's arms were full, fleshy and strong – just like the rest of her. And Joe had put on a bit over the years as well.

'Phil was down the Wellington. He says, can we come to him 'n' Angie's on Saturday night for dinner?'

'I'll have to speak to her about that myself. It'll depend what she's cooking.'

'What she's cooking? Oh, no. Maureen, you're not going on a bloody diet again?!'

'Look who's talking. You could do with taking off a few pounds.'

'We're not talking about me. I don't see why you have to diet. It makes you miserable, you put it all back on again afterwards, and anyway, I like you just the way you are. At least there's something to get hold of of a night.'

'Cheeky! And I'm not listening. In two months I'm going to be fifty and we're bound to have a big do. I want a new dress and I'm going to look good in it. Any road, I miss the girls from Slim-Plicity. I haven't seen

Frances for ages and we did have such a laugh. Do you want the ice-cream in the freezer or shall I have it?'

Maureen lay on her back under the duvet and listened to Joe's tiny, gasping snores. She ruffled what was left of his hair and sighed contentedly. She could see herself, on her fiftieth birthday, in one of those posh cocktail dresses walking into the back room of the Wellington, Heyside High Street, on Joe's arm, and all eyes turning. Angie, her eldest daughter, and Phil would be there, of course, but they would have to get someone to look after the babies. Oh, she could just eat that Kelly and Jason. The most gorgeous grandchildren anyone could wish for. Chris would bring Lisa; she'd got used to them living together though Eccles was a bit far away, and Sharon of course was still at home – if you could call it that – she was never in. Sharon would help her on her diet, as she does nutrition at college, and she's always on at her Mum to lose weight. Says she's embarrassed, she does. Teenagers! Maureen felt round and solid, lying in bed, safe and protected by all that flesh. Still, it would have to go.

And she would have fun. There was a great crowd at Slim-Plicity and Stella really did inspire you. She remembered one Thursday night when she'd only lost half a pound, Viv had stayed the same and Frances had put on two, and they were all so pig-sick that they decided to go for an Indian. And the waiter gave them a table by the window, and there they were, eating their poppadams and onion bhajis, when Viv sees Stella coming up the street and the three of them – honest to God – dived below the table and the whole restaurant looked round! It was one of the best nights she'd had for ages! I could just do with an onion bhaji right now, thought Maureen.

Sandra held down her onion bhaji with her fork and used her knife to cut it in half, revealing the spicy orange-yellow interior. She swallowed one half, and looked around this Indian vegetarian restaurant in Cheetham Hill. It was unlicensed; the restaurant was basic but clean, with scrubbed wooden tables, and devoid of the usual flock wallpaper and monotonous piped music. It was Cathy's idea to come here, and she had to admit it was a good one. She was rather looking forward to the next course, which was to be a sag paneer, a sort of spinach curry with cheese, and a stuffed paratha – which was fried naan bread. All very fattening, no doubt. Which reminded her of what she wanted to talk about to Cathy. Cathy was one of Sandra's closest friends at the university, although she didn't do English Literature, like Sandra, but Psychology.

'Cathy, would you say I was fat?'

'Well, how would you define "fat"?'

'Look, I'm fatter than you at any rate. You seem to be able to eat anything and you're positively sylph-like!'

'I've got a high metabolic rate. And we all love you the way you are, Sandra. I know lots of people fatter than you. Why worry?'

'Why worry?! Because I'm thoroughly miserable about it all. I'm five foot six inches and eleven and a half stone, and it's going up. I'm the only student I know who doesn't wear jeans because my thighs are like tree trunks. In all these Indian skirts and baggy blouses I look like a refugee from a bazaar! They don't make a bra with a cup size big enough to fit me and wobbly bits stick out from the sides. I take extra large in tights and I'm only twenty. And I've got stretch marks on my stomach. Stretch marks!'

'You sound as if you really dislike yourself, Sandra. Your self-esteem is really low.'

'Well, of course, I'm fat.'

'And you're beating yourself up about it. Can't you try to love yourself the way you are right now?'

'Yes, but when I look in the mirror all I can see are these mountains of flesh.'

'You must thank your body for everything it does for you. Tell it how much you appreciate it. Write it all down in the form of a letter!'

'Yes, but I'd feel a proper fool doing that.'

'Sandra! Be assertive with yourself!'

'Yes, but –'

'I knew it! You're playing "Yes, but". It's a game. It comes from TA – transactional analysis. Sorry, I'm not making myself clear. Some people, people who basically have low self-esteem, reinforce this negative image they have of themselves by refusing to accept help from others. So they play "Yes, but". All advice is met by objections. You see, you don't WANT to be helped.'

'Crap.'

'No, listen. Love yourself, and you'll be open to what I'm saying. You're being negative. You think that everyone else is okay, but you're not okay. That's from TA too. Lots of people are like it. "I'm not okay, you're okay".'

'I suppose that does describe me a bit. I'm hardly my own best friend.'

'That's it, Sandra! Look, have you read *Fat is a Feminist Issue*? I'll lend it to you. And I know this woman – Liz Breen – from the Women's Group. She co-ordinates a Fat Women's Support Group. It meets in Heyside on a Thursday. I'll get you the details. Oh, here's our sag paneer. Spinach is very good for you – full of iron. Especially good for women . . .'

Sandra Coverdale cycled home to her shared house in Middleton, her bicycle lamp swinging perilously behind her. So, she thought, I'm not okay. Basically I don't like myself. Could be. And if fat is a feminist issue maybe I'm not fat, just oppressed. Worth finding out about. It's hard work riding this bike. Huh! Like Falstaff – 'lards the lean earth as he walks along . . .' Oh, that this too, too solid flesh would melt! That's what Shakespeare says about obesity. All the over-weight characters I can think of in the whole of English Literature are comic. The Wife of Bath, Parson Adams, Pickwick. Being Fat is Bad News. There! I'm beating myself up again. Cathy's right. No, she isn't. It's not healthy to be fat – riding this bike's sheer agony – and even size sixteens don't quite fit me.

Sandra padlocked her bike to the railings and un-locked the front door. She looked in the stained and spotted hall mirror. She saw her bloated stomach and grimaced. She ignored her dark, attractive eyes, her contemporary spiky hair. The tears welled up. At the

14

top of the landing a light coming out of the door facing informed her that Mark was still awake. She had to talk to someone.

'Mark?'

'Sandra? Come in. I'll take a break from the essay. I've got two more nights.'

Sandra liked Mark's room. It was the smallest room in the three-bedroomed house, and only contained a narrow bed, a desk, a rail for hanging clothes, piles upon piles of books, and an array of left-wing posters, dominated by the large likeness of Che Guevara, a family heirloom passed down from Mark's oldest brother.

'Mark, I'm suicidal.'

'Is it Dave?'

'No, it's me. I'm so fat.'

'It's not your fault. You can't help it. Western obesity is only one reflection of the socio-economic base. Affluence in capitalist society inevitably leads to the concentration of nutritional resources in one small part of society. You're a victim. The food's there, you eat it.'

'You make me sound like a pig!'

'We all are. Such is capitalism. Give it up. Join the Workers' Revolutionary Party. Lenin wasn't fat.'

'You don't understand!'

Sandra was back in her room, which overlooked the back garden. Things were reaching a crisis. Now where did she put the chocolate? Was it behind the George Eliot? Think! Of course. It's behind the T. S. Eliot – *The Waste Land*. She curled up on her bean bag and unwrapped the Double Decker. She ate it quickly in case Mark came up to see if she was all right. He didn't. She ate the Toblerone. Her stomach hurt and filled with an anger and bitterness difficult to express. She would read. Nothing heavy. Here was the local paper. And she saw . . .

'Slim-Plicity'

(Oh, God! How naff! Can't they think of a better pun than that?)

'Are those extra pounds getting you down?'

(You could say that.)

'Are you sick of bingeing?'

(Yes.)

'So come on down to Slim-Plicity!

The answer is simple.

Not one of us can do it alone.

But together . . .

WE'RE OKAY!'

Okay again . . . Could I feel okay? Cathy said I didn't. Maybe this is what I need . . . the support of other women . . . When does it say . . .? Tomorrow, Thursday – oh, damn! The same night as the Fat Women's Support Group. I'm going to have to go to one of them . . .

Judith stubbed out her cigarette in the wooden ashtray, and the acrid smoke mingled with the scent of burning wood. She looked up at the clock. Ten past twelve. It interested her how she was no longer hungry at lunch-time. Since losing her excess weight her appetite had shrunk too, and she seemed not to need food. And tonight, of course, she would score Bull's-eye. It would be the culmination of everything. And she was meeting

16

Geoff afterwards. Her stomach knotted and her thighs felt weak. No, she was not hungry, and she would skip lunch.

The other girls had left the office ten minutes ago and the only sound was the rushing of traffic in the street below. Alone, Judith fell into a familiar reverie, a series of mental tableaux.

Three weeks ago she was immersed in typing a complicated document. There was a tap on her shoulder. It was Geoff Hirst from Small Claims. She hadn't seen him for about a year. As she turned, she saw his face move from lack of recognition, through confusion, to a frank appreciation of her as – joy of joys – a sex object! Her answering smile echoed his. She was a siren, a nymph, Marilyn Monroe . . . He left his hand on her shoulder a fraction too long.

'They said I'd find Judith Pearce down here?'

'That's me.'

'I thought . . . haven't I?'

She assumed the manner of the Mona Lisa: inscrutable, knowing. That was their first meeting.

The wind swept through Judith's hair, and it streamed out as she stood on the deck of the SS Ruritania, *leaning on the rails and looking out over the ocean. From behind, a strong, certain touch smoothed her wild auburn locks, and she turned, to be clasped and lost in the warm, protective, smouldering embrace of Captain Geoffrey Hirst . . .*

Two nights later she was packing her bag to leave the office rather late, when Geoff came in. He sat on the edge of her desk and they talked. He lived in Oldham. He was twenty-six. He supported Manchester City. And he was married. But not happily. Her heart sunk, until she remembered (strange she should have forgotten) that she was married too, and it was interesting how she had hardly given Len a thought.

That night, it was surprisingly easy to leave some food on her plate at the end of the meal, as Stella had always instructed them to do, because she was simply not hungry. Len was out in the mini-cab that evening and she went upstairs into their bedroom and looked in the mirror. She saw herself differently. Her hair was seductive, really she had very attractive brown eyes, and there could be no doubt about it – she was slim. She ran her hands down the sides of her body. The bulges were all gone. She could actually feel her own hands through her body. She felt sexy. Her intense curiosity drove her to remove her jeans and sweater. She looked at herself semi-naked. She was petite, slim and sexy. She tried to see herself with Geoff's eyes. Waves of excitement beat in her. And then she was embarrassed. She put on her dressing-gown and went downstairs.

The next day she had to type a very complicated document for Geoff. When she'd finished, he came down from the fifth floor and said, 'You've typed that very well, but then you're a very talented lady ...' What could he have meant?

Judith Pearce, the fetching parlourmaid of Cassland Hall, was dusting in the drawing-room when the handsome master of the house, Sir Geoffrey Hirst, crept up behind her. He covered her eyes with his sinewy hands.

'Guess who, you ravishing beauty?'

'Unhand me, sir!'

He grasped her waist and swung her round to face

18

*him. She swooned in his rough, powerful embrace,
and melted in ecstasy as his mustachioed lips bruised
hers.*

Geoff had a moustache. His hair was sandy coloured
and his eyes were grey. He drove a Y reg. blue Fiesta
and liked Dire Straits. They always had long conversations now when he brought her work. She did all his
typing. His wife didn't understand him. He thought
Judith was beautiful and he said he liked slim women.
Judith lost four pounds that week and was the Star
Slimmer. She won some bath salts.

*High up in his penthouse flat Geoffrey Hirst III, the
multi-millionaire deftly undid the straps of Judi's fine
silk brassière. Her breasts fell free and his masterly hands
caressed them . . .*

Then it was Barbara's leaving do down at the Dog
and Duck. She was leaving to have a baby and nearly
everyone came to wish her the best, as she was a good
sort. The typing pool had bought her a changing mat
and layette basket from Boots. And Judith had found
herself on a corner table with Geoff. Her one glass of
dry white had gone to her head, as she hadn't
eaten for hours. Every time she spoke to him she
touched him. His foot found hers below the table.
Their knees approached more closely. And they talked.
He really liked her. He couldn't stop thinking about
her. He'd tried but it was no use. Could he see her for
a whole evening? And Judith agreed. After Slim-Plicity
meetings she often went out with one or more of the
girls, and Len neither knew nor cared about it. She
arranged to see Geoff after the next meeting.

Sheikh Geoffrey Hirst strode into the harem and his

19

eyes immediately met those of the slender, small-framed Judith. He signalled to his eunuchs. They brought her to his chambers and with her accustomed art she slowly removed each thin samite veil. She stood naked in front of him, modest in her stance, but self-assured. He gazed, lost in admiration of her ivory skin, her small, firm breasts, and that triangle of auburn hair. He pulled her towards him and violently they . . .

'Judith, aren't you having any lunch?'

'What? . . . Er . . . no, it's Slim-Plicity tonight, Tracey. And I might score Bull's-eye.'

'Well, I think you're looking a bit peaky. I'd have something substantial if I were you,' suggested Tracey, biting a half moon into her tuna and mayonnaise sandwich. Judith looked at the food with distaste and lit another St Moritz. Eight and a half hours before she would see Geoff.

She had fallen asleep during her relaxation tape. As she came to consciousness she automatically pressed her hands down on her stomach to reassure herself that it was still flat. It was. She lay still on her back and collected her thoughts, her eyes closed. This morning the scales had told her that she was nine stone one. That was acceptable but it would be safer to be just under the nine stone. She would slip back into third gear for a week, and miss that meal with Richard. It was Thursday today, and now it was late afternoon. Tonight was Heyside, and she would wear her navy pin-stripe suit with a fresh white blouse. It was important to look smart, slim, not particularly sexy, and very much in control. Stella knew her job well.

Stella Martin, thirty-one years old, was a full-time instructor for Slim-Plicity. Eight years ago she joined one of the first Slim-Plicity groups and lost three and a half stone. She kept up her association with the group both formally and informally, and in time trained to be an instructor. Her success and ever-increasing commitment to Slim-Plicity led her to leave her position as personnel officer for a High Street bank and to concentrate exclusively on slimming. She now led four slimming groups in the north-west, and was tipped for promotion when Area Co-ordinator became vacant.

Stella swung her legs on to the carpet and stood in front of the cheval mirror that occupied a prominent position in her bedroom. She gave herself a critical examination. Bust okay. Waist good. Hips still jut out just a little too much. Bottom needs tightening. She looked at her face. Needs make-up. Now.

Stella's short, dark hair was well cut, and framed a heart-shaped face with finely chiselled features. Her brown eyes were intelligent, and this was somehow enhanced by the worry lines on her forehead. Her nose was regular, and her lips just that little bit too full. Her skin was clear but pale.

Stella clipped her hair back and applied a small amount of moisturizer to her face. Then from a squat glass bottle she shook out the remains of her foundation (must remember to get some more) and massaged it on to her skin. Her mind wandered. She hoped it would be a good night at Heyside. Anne Sargeant's groups were doing well recently, and Stella loathed the way she would bring this into the conversation almost as an aside. Or often she would praise Stella, somehow implying that she could afford to do this as Stella was junior to her. Nearly every encounter she had with Anne, despite their official friendship, left her feeling strangely inadequate. She smoothed the cream down into her neck, and then dabbed her face with translucent powder.

She brushed highlighter on her eyelids. It was rumoured that Jo McKenzie might be coming to England. Jo was Stella's inspiration. She rubbed in a dark brown shadow along her socket. It was Jo who had founded Slim-Plicity in the States twelve years ago. She was fifteen stone and felt intimidated by the other slimming groups. She needed a more informal and friendly support network. She gathered a band of women around her and together they lost all their excess weight and started this world-wide chain of slimming groups. Stella put a shimmering white powder just under her eyebrow. Now for a thin line painted above and below her lashes. How wonderful it must have been to actually found an organization like Slim-Plicity, and to be ultimately responsible now for all these thousands of women whose lives have been transformed by their dramatic weight losses. She took her false eyelashes out of the drawer, having already applied two coats of black mascara. She'd seen recent pictures of Jo. Her figure was elfin, and she seemed ageless. What an inspiration. Now Stella finished off with some blusher, and her efficient red lipstick. Done. Inspect. Quite satisfactory.

She put on the kimono that Richard had brought back from Japan on his last business trip. She would wear this until it was time to change into her suit, and she went into the spare bedroom to glance through her Slim-Plicity files. There on the desk was an unopened letter from HQ that Stella had completely forgotten about. With pleasurable anticipation she sat down and tore open the envelope. She read the contents with intense interest. Slim-Plicity were having an autumn promotion. The group which achieved the greatest average weight loss per person over the next eight weeks would celebrate with a buffet and presentation at the Carlton International Hotel. Delightful. And the winning instructor would receive a fifty-pound voucher to be spent at Kendal Milne's (better not tell the groups that) and a dinner with Jo McKenzie, who was coming to England after all. Jo McKenzie! Stella's heart beat quickly. She had worshipped no one as she had worshipped Jo. All through the months she lost her excess weight she carried on imaginary conversations with Jo at night. Jo was her idol, her mother, her best friend. Jo's eyes assured her she could do it. Jo's smile – which beamed at them from the poster which adorned all Slim-Plicity meetings – promised her happiness at the end. She ran her groups as if she were Jo McKenzie.

And now there was the chance of meeting Jo. This was actually more important to her than the honour of winning the promotion and scoring over Anne Sargeant – as pleasant as that would be. The money was of no account. Stella thought about each of her groups with rapidity. Castleford was only a small group and it would put too much strain on the members. Middleton was certainly a possibility but it was an afternoon class, mainly composed of old ladies who tended to lose weight rather more slowly. Ditto for her morning group at Whitelea. That left Heyside. And indeed the prospects were good. The members were chiefly young, and some, like that Judith Pearce, were very committed. Wasn't she about to score Bull's-eye? There were quite a few recent arrivals, and that would make good loss figures. Why not Heyside? She breathed in deeply. She was known for her determination.

By six forty-five Stella Martin stood at her front door, immaculate, car keys in her hand. Her Bull's-eye *diamanté* brooch sparkled on her lapel. But the glint in her eyes was brighter still.

CHAPTER TWO

Propped up against the wall of the Heyside British Legion was a large cardboard notice bearing the legend SLIM-PLICITY WELCOMES YOU. It was only legible to those close to it, as the cloudy evening had already set in. The double doors leading to the entrance hall were held open by two large wooden wedges. On the right were two doors: one decorated with a silhouette of a lady in a crinoline, the other with a gentleman in a dress suit. On the left, another door was slightly ajar, and the muted sound of several conversations indicated that the Slim-Plicity meeting was here. Helen was aware of a faint smell of disinfectant threading itself with stale cigarette smoke. She let Judith go ahead of her and waited hesitantly for some instruction.

'You must go to the new members' table over there and register. You'll be all right. They're ever so nice. I just pay and get weighed. See you soon.'

Judith hurried over to a trestle table and greeted the two women seated behind it. Suddenly cut adrift, Helen paused and orientated herself. Below the stage were three rows of chairs in a semicircle, and in front of these a small square table covered with a green velvet cloth. Behind the table, pinned on to a large screen were four posters. One was of a large, obese woman, dowdily dressed in old-fashioned clothes. The next was of a strawberry sundae. The third repeated Slim-Plicity's newspaper advertisement, and the last appeared to be a four course meal. Helen immediately felt quite hungry.

'Are you a new member, love?'

'Yes. What do I have to do?'

'Just come here and register.'

A middle-aged lady with heavily drawn eyebrows and pointed glasses thrust a sheaf of papers at Helen, and invited her to sit down by a small table, where another young girl was engaged in filling out a similar set of forms. The only writing implement Helen could find in her handbag was a My Little Pony pencil, so she waited until the girl had finished and asked if she could borrow her pen. The girl looked as awkward as she felt and both smiled nervously at each other. Just then came a cry of 'BULL'S-EYE!'

Both Helen and Sandra turned their heads to see Judith being embraced by Stella, and heard the delighted shrieks of the knot of women around the scales. Helen felt that to acknowledge her friendship with Judith would spoil the balance of her tentative approach to this girl, so she said nothing. They both smiled again. Helen realized that she must be a student, or something like that. She was dressed in a long, fringed black skirt and a baggy navy T-shirt. Her hair was spiked and her eye make-up heavy. Helen had not expected to see anyone like that at Slim-Plicity. The girl looked ill at ease and rather young. Helen felt slightly maternal. Sandra was conscious of the novelty of talking to a woman who was probably a real housewife from Heyside and not a student. She felt a little daring and a little inadequate. The woman looked about as fat as her, which was encouraging. And she looked quite intelligent too. Perhaps this woman would give her the support and solidarity she was craving. Sandra wondered why she was here; she looked very composed. She was aware of a large shadow, and a third woman joined them.

'Are you the other new members? I'm Maureen. I'm a new member – well, not so new, they all know me here! It's good to be back – you can't do it alone, you know. Not that I've ever done it to the end, reached Bull's-eye, that is. It's a struggle, and that's a fact. But this is the only place you'll do it. Stella's all right. She doesn't shout at you like some of them. She's right enthusiastic. Do you both have families?'

'Two little ones, a boy and a girl. You're not married, are you?' Helen suggested to Sandra, in an attempt to bring her in.

'No. I'm still at university.'

'Ah, you're one of those clever ones. You won't find it hard to diet, then,' asserted Maureen, illogically.

Sandra wished it were true. Sometimes she felt that it was easier for women who didn't question everything, who didn't see two sides to every issue. She felt like Hamlet – to diet, or not to diet. Just now it seemed as if dieting might be the answer. She was aware of something quite hypnotic about the shared assumption of this group of women that it was important, desirable and possible to lose weight. Why else would they all come? She watched Helen hand in her forms, open her purse, and part with a ten-pound note, for which she received little change. Holding a small card, Helen walked towards the scales.

It reminded her a bit of the ante-natal clinic. She

almost expected the group leader to take her blood pressure too. The scales were clinic scales. Helen stood on the rubber base and watched this glamorous, competent woman deftly whizz a metal pointer along a bar marking out stones and pounds.

'That's eleven twelve.'

Helen reddened. Although the leader had whispered this, it seemed rather too public, and rather shocking. She did need to lose weight, then. She stood there guiltily, but the leader was reassuring.

'I'm Stella Martin. Welcome to Slim-Plicity! We'll soon get rid of these extra stones. They're not really you.'

Stella looked down at a table of heights and weights.

'We'll make your Bull's-eye ten stone one. Bull's-eye is your target weight. Don't worry, you'll reach it. Have you been to us before?'

'No. I've never dieted before. It must have been having the children that made me put it on. I've never really lost it.'

'But you will now!' said Stella, cajolingly. Helen found this attractive, intense woman hard to resist.

'Here's your manual. Look through it now before the meeting begins, and then at the end I see the new members to explain it properly. You'll have plenty of support on your first week. Slim-Plicity is the FRIENDLY slimming group!' beamed Stella. She obviously believes it, thought Helen.

Clutching her weighing-in card, her slimming manual, her handbag and her mac, Helen made for the seats. Judith wasn't watching her and Helen did not feel inclined to join her. On the bus on the way here

Judith seemed distant, preoccupied; perhaps she'd regretted asking her along. Helen sat down alone, sinking inadvertently and unwillingly into the red plastic chair she had chosen. She looked around her.

She had never been inside the British Legion before. It was revolting. The walls were painted a bright mustard yellow, and the windows had been bricked in, plastered and painted brown. Over in one corner was the bar, shut now, of course. The beer pump handles and spirit optics skulked guiltily in the dim light, as if they recognized that they were greatly disapproved of by this bunch of healthy, disciplined women. Again Helen's eyes were drawn by the leader's table and the tempting posters of food. And then she watched the other women. Already about sixteen women were seated around her. A large number were smoking with an air of desperation; others were chewing rhythmically. A woman by the side of her seemed to be chewing the side of her cheek. Two women sat alone and looked serious, introspective. Near them a group of ladies sat avidly reading the manual. An air of expectation was almost tangible.

The student came and sat down next to her.

'Hello again. My name's Sandra. What's yours?'

'Helen. What do you study at the university?'

'English Literature. I'm in my second year.'

'I liked English when I was at school. I was quite good at it.'

But Sandra was not here to talk about literature. She changed the subject.

'Have you belonged to a slimming club before?'

'No. This is my first time. My neighbour comes here. In fact she's reached Bull's-eye tonight.'

'This is my first slimming club too. I'm eleven ten. I'm so disgusted with myself I'm just going to have to do something about it. It's a good idea, the group support, don't you think? Obesity is such an isolating experience. I'm quite excited about this. I'm going to read my manual now.'

Helen liked Sandra's enthusiasm. Isolating. That's an interesting word. Was she isolated? The idea made her uncomfortable, and she dismissed it. She tried to listen to the conversations around her.

'That looks nice!'

'Look! You can have baked beans again this week.'

'Trouble is, I'm not really a fish person myself.'

'You can have Kwik Save crispbread.'

'Can you? I thought that was over the gear limit.'

'No, they're only seventy. But they taste like poly-styrene. They're not worth having anyway.'

'I had a lovely lunch on Sunday. My sister came round and first we had half a grapefruit each, then some of the Slim-Plicity starter soup, then some prawns in a salad and a piece of fruit . . .'

'Well, at least I stayed the same; it's better than putting it on!'

'I'm starving!'

'All I've got left tonight is one fruit.'

'When I get home I'm pigging out good and proper. It's not like you're cheating on a Thursday night.'

'He brought home fish, chips, peas and a bottle of Vimto.'

'Half a pound of Dairy Box . . .'

'You grill the mince so the fat runs out . . .'

Helen felt very, very hungry. She had never heard

30

so much discussion of food, every sort of food, in her whole life. And now that she was about to do without it she realized how much she was going to miss it. She felt even hungrier. Sandra was still immersed in the manual. She watched Maureen coming to sit at the end of the row, and realized that the talking was dying down. She turned to watch Stella leave the scales and stride purposefully to the green table in front of Helen. For a very brief moment Helen felt she was little again, sitting in the classroom at the beginning of a lesson. Or was it church she was thinking of? But the dynamic woman standing in front of her looked more like an executive, in a pin-striped suit with expensive jewellery. How wonderful and impossible to be like that!

'Good evening, ladies! Our losses this week total thirty-six pounds, and we've put on seven. That's mainly because a number of you are expecting your periods. But well done anyway. The biggest single loss this week was five pounds – yes, that's you, Heather! Heather Barnett, come and get this week's mystery prize.'

A large middle-aged lady wrapped up in a dark green coat moved out from the back of the group with the daintiness of a ballerina. She accepted a small cylindrical parcel, and opened it to reveal a Body Shop lotion. Still mystified, she smiled shyly at the other women, and returned to her seat.

'We have one Bull's-eye tonight – Judith Pearce. Since joining us eight months ago Judith has lost forty-six pounds. I can't tell you how proud I am of you, Judith. Tell the group, did you ever deviate from the manual?'

31

'No, Stella. I could see it was working for me.'

'And how do you feel tonight?'

'Fantastic. I feel as if I've been born again. The excitement's with you all day.'

'Do you think you could have done it without us?'

'No, Stella. I needed the support and encouragement.'

'You see? We can do it together. Slim-Plicity works. And you thoroughly deserve your success, Judith. Enjoy yourself!'

I will, thought Judith.

'We have three new members tonight. Where's Sandra Coverdale?'

'Here.'

'Welcome, Sandra. What made you join us?'

'I saw your ad in the paper. And I don't want to be fat any more.'

'Then you're in the right place. Get in gear with Slim-Plicity. Where's Helen Greenwood? Ah, next to Sandra. You came with Judith, didn't you?'

Helen nodded. Stella sensed her embarrassment and quickly moved on.

'I'm sure you'll do just as well. Welcome back, Maureen! No more pie and pea suppers for you, my dear.'

'You're all right, Stella. I'm going to be a good girl this time.'

'Now, I'd like to ask the new members to take a look at the blown-up picture on the right. That was me eight years ago. Yes, there's quite a difference, isn't there? Eight years ago I was permanently depressed and neurotic about my weight. Then I had the good fortune to read about Jo McKenzie in a magazine. Jo, like me, was overweight; overweight and miserable. She comes from the States. She was a harassed housewife, always caring for others, cooking for others, never out of the kitchen. And try as she might, she could never lose weight. Then one morning, when her husband was in the office and the kids at school, and she was alone and feeling at an all-time low, she decided to take action. Using her children's paints and crayons, she drew posters that she displayed all round town; on the school gates, in the laundromat, even in BurgerBar! She asked for the help of other women in the same predicament as herself. And soon there was a response. First just a trickle of women joined her, than a few more. Jo wrote to renowned nutritionists to ask their advice in writing the manual. And within a few months she'd lost all her excess weight, and so had her buddies. That was the beginning of Slim-Plicity, ladies. And it works just as well in England today. That's because we at Slim-Plicity understand each other.

'We understand that we are different from a lot of other people. We have a problem with food. We don't eat only when we're hungry, but for other reasons: we eat when we're bored, or when we're lonely; when we're depressed or suffering from premenstrual tension; when we're stressed or anxious. Call it greed, call it compulsive eating, call it what you will – we all recognize the syndrome. It is only when we can control our uncontrollable appetites that we will lose weight. The manual tells you what to eat, and Slim-Plicity members will tell you how to eat. Right! Get into your Buddy groups.'

'What on earth . . .' began Helen.

'You new members, form a Buddy group of your own, and, Judith, you join them to show them how it works. Buddy groups are smaller units in the large group so you can share your problems in a more intimate way. No other slimming group has this! Tonight I want you to discuss between yourselves, and then tell me what YOU do when hunger strikes and you don't want to eat. Share your tips in the group and then report back to me!'

Maureen slid along the row of chairs to join Helen and Sandra. Judith walked over and drew up her chair so she was sitting in front of them. Helen became aware of the sound of talk from other surrounding groups, and she looked at Judith, waiting for her to take the lead.

'I find a bath always helps,' suggested Judith, 'or having a face pack. You know, the sort that dries on your face so that you can't move a muscle. What about you, Helen?'

'I haven't really tried not eating if I'm hungry. I suppose that's where this extra weight comes from. I don't know.'

Sandra leapt in.

'If I'm hungry I'll go and visit a friend, or go out for a walk. If I stay in my room I'm bound to eat. Is that the kind of thing she wants us to say?'

'You say what you like, my love. Stella's a good sort but you've got to admit there are times when you have to eat. I'm going through my change of life and when I get depressed I've got to have something sweet. I'm partial to those Cadbury's Chocolate Eclairs or a Mars bar. I've tried raw carrots but it's not the same.'

'I know, Maureen, but they're not in the manual,' said Judith a shade smugly. 'Have you tried the Nutrasweet mint chocolate drinks? They're only forty calories each.'

'Where can you get them?' asked Sandra anxiously.

'Sainsbury's sell double sachets, or . . . ssh! She's starting again.'

Stella clapped her hands to bring the groups to attention. From behind the screen she had produced a flip chart and she now stood, armed with a large felt-tip marker, ready to accept suggestions from her audience.

'Right! Fire away! Doing word-search puzzles, good, Joan . . . Drinking plain hot water, thanks, Mavis . . . Having a bath, that's a good one, Judith . . . A glass or two of wine? No, Maureen, that'll put the weight back on . . . Going out, well done, Sandra . . . Knitting! Lovely . . . Any more? What are you lot giggling about at the back? Don't tell me! But you're absolutely right. You can't eat while you're doing it and it burns up two hundred calories a time. Don't blush, Judith, we're all girls here! Seriously, though, I'd like to add some tips. Remember that we are all of us near a phone. When your willpower's low, ring a buddy. Or ring me. At Slim-Plicity we support each other. Jo's friends supported her. When I was near giving it all up I thought of Jo, and what she suffered, and it inspired me. I stuck a picture of Jo McKenzie inside my fridge and so she was always there, spurring me on. Jo suffered so that you can lose weight today!' Stella breathed in deeply.

'Tonight I have some very exciting news. But before

35

I give it to you, we'll do the titbits session. I want news, tips, recipes, boasts and even – dare I say it – confessions! Who's first?'

'What do you do if you're constipated, Stella?'

'Be patient. It'll come. Eat your All-Bran for breakfast, and plenty of wholemeal bread. Try baked beans but check the sugar content on the label. Yes, Mary?'

'I went to a party on the weekend, Stella, and I wouldn't even go in the room where the food was. I'm in third gear at the moment so I had my one glass of wine and then stuck to Slimline tonics. But I still put on this week,' wailed a tall blonde girl from the middle.

'It's your period, dear. It'll show up next week; you'll lose twice as much. Ethel?'

'I had a lovely lunch on Saturday. My sister came round and first we had half a grapefruit each, then some of the Slim-Plicity starter soup, then some prawns in a salad and a piece of fruit. When my cousin came round the next . . .'

'Lovely, Ethel, aren't you doing well?'

'Mine's a confession, Stella,' came the next voice. 'I was in the house by myself on Saturday. He'd taken the lads to football. I was just ravenous. I went to the freezer, and I didn't just have a quarter of a pizza' – dramatic pause – 'but half a pizza. Half a pizza! You know, the Giant Supreme ones.'

'But you didn't eat it all, Karen. And that's because you know you've got to come here and get weighed. Which shows it works. And that you need us. We all need each other. And now for my news . . .

'Headquarters have sent me details of a new promotion. Over the next eight weeks each Slim-Plicity group in the north-west will add up its total weight loss, subtracting gains, and divide it by the number of women in the group, so we get an average weight loss each week. The group with the best average weight loss per person is invited to the Carlton International Hotel for a special slimmers' evening buffet, and you'll all be allowed a glass of champagne – dry, of course.'

The group were impressed. Mutters of approval rose from the floor.

'So all we have to do is be the best group in the north-west. Which of course we already are!' said Stella, with more enthusiasm than truth. 'New members, we are relying on you to start us off with a bang next week, as the first week always results in a good loss. And to all of you, have a splendid week. Drive carefully!'

Helen heard the faint sound of stomachs rumbling. Buttocks shifted and women checked their watches. The majority of the women put on their coats and left, some quickly; others stopped to chat. Judith tapped Helen on the shoulder and effectively stopped her observations.

'Look, Helen, I can't come home with you tonight. I'm meeting some girls from the office. It's Barbara's leaving do!' she said, with a flash of inspiration.

'I wish you'd told me before. I'm not very keen on travelling alone at night.'

'I'm sorry. I'm sure you'll be all right.'

Judith felt a momentary pang of guilt. It passed. She pecked Helen on the cheek in a mist of heavy musk perfume, and disappeared hastily through the

door. Stella was on hand to dispel Helen's spec-
ulations.

'Time for the manual now, girls. Are you sitting
comfortably? At Slim-Plicity we don't like to talk of
dieting, which can sound rather grim. So we talk about
driving – it's more positive. People with drive get there
in the end. So for your starter week you're in first
gear. It's a fairly stringent eating plan, but well worth
the effort. Turn to page three. See how there are different coloured food groups. Green foods are go, go, go!
They include vegetables, citrus fruits and a number
of low or no-calorie foods. You can eat as many as
you like of these. Amber Ones are proteins, like fish,
cheese, eggs, meat, beans and you can have five units a
day. The unit quantities are listed at the back of the
manual. Amber Twos are carbohydrates such as bread,
rice, potatoes and pasta. Only two units of those a day,
girls. You can have three units of Amber Threes which
are fats – butter, margarine. Red foods are of course
forbidden. But from second gear onwards I will give
you a calorie allowance per week so that you can choose
a treat from this list. It's not all doom and gloom. Also
in your manual you'll find daily menu suggestions with
a weekly shopping list to help you plan your personal
programme. You'll also find a diary that I want you
to use. Write down everything that you eat there so
that I can check that you've got the hang of it. Any
questions?'

Maureen had several, and they were specific and
complicated. Sandra was studying her manual earn-
estly. Helen felt suddenly resentful. Why should
anyone tell her just what she was to eat? It all seemed

such a lot of fuss and bother. And such an infringement of her liberty. She felt rebellious, like a schoolgirl. And yet, what a novelty to put herself first for a change. She'd have to plan the family's meals around her. Would she dare to do it? Would Tony mind? Probably not. What could she have for breakfast tomorrow?

'Do you need any help with the manual, Helen?'

'No, Stella, I think I'll be all right. I've got Judith next door if I need her.'

'Of course. And my number's printed on the back of the manual. I'm looking forward to seeing how you all get on next week.' Stella beamed at them, and walked over to the ladies at the desks to wind up proceedings. The three new members put on their coats and left together. Outside there was a faint drizzle and the lights from the Wellington looked particularly inviting. The three were reluctant to depart, gripped by that strange inertia that affects people on the brink of leave-taking.

'Are you coming for a drink and a packet of crisps, loves? There's no need to start tonight, you know. You may as well enjoy yourselves while you can.'

'Sorry, Maureen. My husband will worry if I'm home later than I said. Maybe another time. My bus is due in fifteen minutes.'

'I'll come in with you, Maureen, as I'm joining some people who are having a meeting upstairs. But I've got to go straight up there.'

'No, it's all right, dear. It doesn't matter. There's an off-licence opposite my house, and I promised Joe I'd bring him back summat. Be good!'

Maureen opened her umbrella and waddled off into the distance. It was Sandra's turn to go.

'Bye, Helen. I've enjoyed meeting you. Didn't you find it all very inspiring? I did. I'm going to try ever so hard this week. The support makes so much difference. I'll ring you like you said if I get into trouble. Bye!'

Helen watched Sandra cross the pelican, and get swallowed up by the Wellington. A political meeting, no doubt, she thought. Something left-wing. Mind you, I've always voted Labour. Helen thought that it must be fun to be a student. Something was irritating her. Now what was it? Ah, yes – Judith. Fancy going off like that. Rather selfish. I liked Stella; she was very impressive. But I've never heard so much talk of food in all my life – just the very thing you thought these women would want to get away from! And nothing is more tedious than hearing what other people ate for dinner.

She had reached the bus station and was alone at the bus stop, one of several along a huge glass colonnade. She caught a glimpse of her reflection on the side of the shelter. She was shapeless, and when the features of her face were not clear, she could almost pass for middle aged. In the mood for consolation she opened her handbag, ostensibly to get her fare, and found, as she had expected, her emergency supply of Polo mints. Three or four had already gone. She unwrapped the foil from the tube to reveal one white mint with its familiar embossed lettering. On a sudden impulse, she threw the whole tube into the nearby bin.

I might as well begin now, she thought.

CHAPTER THREE

Judith checked her watch against the clock on the tower of St Mary's, Heyside. 9.06 p.m. She glanced nervously around her. Recognizing no one, she turned right, breathing rapidly, and hurried along the now deserted street. She took the first turn on her left, walked past a bus shelter, and then a little further along, parked on the opposite side of the road, was a blue Fiesta, registration number RND 178Y. That could stand for randy, she thought, and giggled. She crossed the road before she reached the car, licked her dry lips, and stood by the passenger door. It opened. She slid inside, and the car roared into action. A cassette was pushed into a thin aperture; Dire Straits asked Judith and Geoff 'Why Worry?'

Why indeed? The slightly narcotic effect of driving along dark roads only semi-familiar, feeling safe from detection, and that melting sensation that both of them shared when close to each other; all these were quite relaxing. Geoff took the road through Rochdale and towards Littleborough; he continued to drive on; they said little. They reached the Craven Heifer at the top of Blackstone Edge.

Geoff opened the door and ushered Judith in. They both looked anxiously around them, scanning the few faces in the lounge.

'What would you like? I'll get them. You find us a seat.'

'Just a dry white wine.'

Judith chose the circular table at the back of the small lounge, since it faced the door. She sat behind it on the wooden settle, and put her handbag on the floor between her feet. Having once looked around the lounge, she decided it was better to be incognito, but she couldn't resist stealing a look at Geoff at the bar. He wore denims, and a long-sleeved striped casual top. She had never seen him out of his office clothes before. He looked younger; almost vulnerable. And he was so good-looking, like a young Charles Dance. Yes, there certainly seemed to be something tragic about him . . .

The fierce revolutionaries, ugly in their filthy green jackets, pulled along their prisoner, Prince Geoffrey. He looked around him agonizingly for one face, and – thank God – saw Judith, disguised in the crowd. Clutching the stiletto in her right hand, with a sudden spring she leapt forward, cutting his bonds, and they ran headlong into the crowd, where . . .

'Here we are, Jude. At last.'

She took a large gulp of her wine from the goblet with a white Plimsoll line etched near the top. Geoff took a long draught of his lager.

'Did it work all right? You got out okay?'

'Yes. Len left before me and he won't be back till late.'

'Same here. Tell me, what do you do at this club of yours?'

'It's a slimming club. Slim-Plicity. You see, I used to be fat, then I joined Slim-Plicity, and I lost it all. All my fat. I scored Bull's-eye tonight. It's the most important night of my life. For months and months I've worked for this. And I feel as if I'm born again. I suppose this sounds silly to you, but I do want you to know about it.'

'No, you're not silly. That's wonderful, Jude. I admire you for that – it's important for a woman to be slim. Come here.'

He put his arm around her waist. Now they felt close. Everything was slipping away from Judith very, very quickly. She finished her wine. For a moment they were both still, reluctant to move. Then Geoff got up, took their empty glasses, and returned to the bar.

Now he sat so close to her that Judith could feel all of his leg next to hers. It was hard to concentrate on what he was saying.

'You're special, you know that? It isn't just the way you look but I feel I can talk to you. We like the same things, don't we? We've got things in common.'

She stroked his thigh. Very daring.

'I can't concentrate when you do that. Judith, I want you to know that it's over between Emma and me. Can I tell you about it?'

'Go on.'

'I met her at Rascals three years ago. She's a librarian. I married her ten months later. In the beginning it worked out – I never changed! But she did. She got in with a bunch of these women's libbers. You're not one, are you?'

'No. I've no time for that.'

Geoff squeezed her hand. 'She started reading all these books, and she went to meetings with other women. She's never been what you would call slim, and she even stopped wearing a bra. She said it was an instrument of depression ... or something. She stopped cleaning the house; she stopped ironing my shirts; I even had to take turns with the shopping.'

'Oh, you poor thing. She didn't look after you!'

'And she put weight on. And then one night she accused me of being a rapist!'

Judith edged away.

'She said men control women through violence, and every man could be a rapist, and so I could be one. That was the last straw. And then the next week when I went down to the typing pool I saw you.'

'Geoff, it's the same for me, really. I don't mean Len's a women's libber, no, I mean we've grown apart. You'd think he would be proud of me, losing all this weight, and it's been the opposite. He used to tempt me with food, and complain we never went out for meals any more. And he stopped talking, and said we couldn't afford the subscription to my health club. And he stopped ... well, you know.'

Judith blushed furiously.

'So have we, Jude. She read this book where it said that sex was also an instrument of depression. But I couldn't anyway. She's over fourteen stone now.'

'My poor love. How awful.'

'This is serious between us, Jude, you know that?'

'Yes.'

It was late. They put on their jackets and left the pub. They drove silently down Blackstone Edge. Below them, all of Rochdale glittered in the cold night air. Judith felt utterly detached from the rest of her life.

She was free. Geoff suddenly turned the car to the left, and pulled to a halt in a lay-by; the car was exposed on the moors, but free from observation.

Their kisses were desperate, hungry and painful. It was just as good as Judith had imagined. She had never been desired like this before, and for the first time in her life she actively responded to a man. She was supremely conscious of her own body, firm and slim. Geoff's hands found her breasts. Thank God she was wearing a bra! The gear stick cut into her, and, like a searchlight, an approaching car's headlamps on full beam exposed their passion.

'No, no not that. Not tonight, Geoff. It's not right here.'

'Judith, I've been waiting ages.'

'Yes, yes, but I can't. Someone might see. It's not right.'

'I love you, Jude.'

'I love you. We will, but not now.'

As they drove silently into Rochdale Judith knew she had been right. She was going to sleep with Geoff, but not in a Fiesta on Blackstone Edge. It was going to be different for her. And Geoff loved her. He said so. And now she was slim. And it was all going to start happening. This new life.

Geoff parked round the corner from Judith's house in Heyside. They were both subdued. They tried to exchange a chaste kiss, but couldn't. And then Judith broke away, in control.

'We will, darling, soon. I promise. Think of me tonight.'

Gently she shut the car door, and hurried along the

road to her own street. Len's car was in the carport and she increased her pace. Momentarily she stopped under a street light and checked her watch. 11.45. Len wouldn't question her. She was safe. Safe, in love, and eight stone seven.

The Wellington was the largest pub in Heyside. In the centre of the spacious ground-floor room was a circular bar, with a dazzling array of bottles, optics and decorated mirrors. Near by, several high tables stood marooned, clung to by groups of drinkers, glad to lean on something solid as their senses blurred. Around the walls were lower tables, with seating, where others conversed and laughed. The fog of cigarette smoke, and insistent throb of the juke-box, made it difficult to discern any one individual with clarity, and so the girl, sitting in the far corner, lost in thought, remained almost unnoticed. She was alone, and her half pint of bitter lay unregarded in front of her. She frowned in concentration, and looked occasionally at her watch.

Sandra was finding it hard to know what to do next. It was her firm intention when leaving home that evening to go to the Fat Women's Support Group too, and then decide which one was going to give her the help she needed. But Stella at Slim-Plicity had done her job very well. Sandra felt quite enthusiastic about dieting – sorry – driving, and couldn't wait to get into first gear. Just imagine being slim and glamorous! It seemed to her as if any weight she lost would count as a real achievement, something concrete, so much more definite than the nebulous satisfaction of a beta-plus for an essay on Elizabethan sonnet sequences.

That was the trouble with studying literature. Yes, of course, it was immensely interesting, and improved your awareness of things, but what good did it do? She never felt she made anything at the end. That was why her father was so doubtful about her course; why hadn't she done law? Well, it would show him if she lost a stone or two. This was illogical, Sandra knew that, but that was how she felt. Dieting was certainly attractive.

And yet, it wasn't so simple. What would her friends say if they knew she had joined Slim-Plicity? It was unthinkable. Cathy would be the first one to try to talk her out of it. Her other feminist friends would also point out that she was making herself into a sex object. Why get slim? To attract a man? And true, she had a steady boyfriend already. Joining Slim-Plicity, in her circle of friends, was as bad as reading *True Romances*, or washing your boyfriend's socks. Her diet would have to be a dark secret. Or perhaps she would be better off going upstairs and listening to what the Fat Women's Support Group had to say. Dialectically she felt at one with them. In a glow of resolution she finished her beer. But what about Helen? She had promised to support Helen through this first week, and this was something she wanted to do. She had never spoken on equal terms before to a woman of Helen's age. Either there was her mother's generation, who talked down to her, or her friends, who were all students too. Helen seemed real. She had a home, children. Sandra would like to get to know her. Or perhaps she could get Helen to come along with her to the Fat Women's Support Group! That was an idea.

She looked down at her watch again. The meeting was probably over by now. Never mind. She would go upstairs and join them.

To the left of Sandra's table was an expansive flight of carpeted stairs. These she ascended and entered the first-floor corridor. Outside the second door on the left was a placard, just saying FWSG. She opened the door gently and looked in. At one end of an oblong conference table sat a huddle of women, talking eagerly. They looked up as they saw her.

'What do you want?'

'Is this the Fat Women's Support Group?' What an embarrassing thing to have to say, thought Sandra, blushing as she spoke.

'Yes. Have you come to join us?'

'I . . . hope so.'

'Look, we're just finishing for tonight,' said the most assertive of the group, 'sit down there, and I'll be with you in a few minutes.'

Sandra did as she was told. She looked around the lavishly oak-panelled room and then stole glimpses of the women seated around the table. The one who was doing most of the talking was certainly fat. About fifteen or sixteen stone, Sandra estimated. She had cut her brown hair very short, and she wore owl-like glasses. The effect was not ugly, as one might imagine. She looked more like a nursery rhyme character, like Tweedledum or Tweedledee. She wore a very large fisherman's smock, and a pair of denim jeans. Yes, she was substantial rather than gross. She leaned forward across the table. Her gestures were extravagant, she smiled freely, and yet one felt she was carried away by her own invective, rather than listening to those around her. Sandra felt attracted to her, but just a little wary, rather as a small rock might feel, alone in a swiftly running stream.

The other women interested her too, and she took full note of them. She had to admit that the woman on the leader's left was not prepossessing. She too had short hair, but had grown one section at the back, which she wore as a short, thin pony-tail. She was red-cheeked and long-nosed. She was covered in a voluminous red knitted sweater, decorated with various badges. A number were familiar to Sandra, as they recounted various feminist slogans, and expressed an interest in the women of Nicaragua. Her eyes were hooded, and unaccountably Sandra felt that she looked dangerous. On the leader's other side sat a very different type of woman. She was fair, and her wispy hair framed a delicately featured but wide face. She wore a large black sweat-shirt, no bra, and black leggings. She should have looked monstrous but she didn't. Even Sandra could see that, but she couldn't work out why. Perhaps, she thought hesitantly, it was because if you felt good about the way you looked, and didn't try to hide yourself, other people might be affected by your confidence. What an encouraging thought! Sandra immediately resolved to buy herself that long-resisted pair of jeans, and to hell with the consequences! The women one by one finished talking, and Sandra could see that the meeting had finished. Chairs were pushed back, and Sandra was invited to join the group round the table. Several of the women put on jackets and left, but Sandra was pleased to see that the three she had been observing were staying to meet her.

The leader stood up.

'Hello. I'm Liz Breen. Sit down and tell us about yourself. Who are you? How did you find out about us? Are you joining?'

Sandra was somewhat taken aback by her forthrightness.

'I'm Sandra Coverdale. I'm a student at the university. Cathy Hogg told me that you met here. I've always had a problem with weight and eating and everything and I just want to attack it from a feminist viewpoint.'

'We're not a slimming club, you know.'

'Oh, no, of course not. I'd like to know more about what you do, really.' Sandra felt a little hesitant, afraid that she might disgrace herself by saying something not quite orthodox. Yet she found these powerful women very attractive, and wanted to prove she could be part of them. But it was probably safer to listen to Liz.

'We're an informal group, and we deliberately have no hierarchy or structure. Recently I've been co-ordinating meetings with Martha,' she indicated the red-cheeked woman, 'and Emma,' the blonde. 'But this could change at any time. Basically we see our position as analogous with gays, blacks, the disabled, or any other oppressed minority. Society has marginalized us and ridicules us. In a world of Page Three models and thin fashion mannequins our only function is to make people laugh. You give me one example of a fat woman in the media, or in films who provides us with a positive image.'

'Yes, I agree. Fat women don't stand a chance.'

'Quite so. Listen, Sandra. When I was your age I used to try to diet. It was hell. I suffered agonies not eating the things I craved. And then one day I woke up and decided to stop dieting and to stay the way I was intended to be. I felt it was my right to choose how I wanted to look. Okay, so I was five stone overweight. But look how much more damage smokers do not only to themselves but to others. Who was I harming?

'And then I began to realize how society – a society run predominantly by men – made it difficult for me. All fashionable clothes stop at size sixteen. Bras are designed for the flat-chested women who don't need them! Fixed tables on Inter-City trains made it impossible for a woman of my size to sit down. Rotating doors prevented me from getting into buildings. I felt excluded, and knew that this was wrong. There was no role-model provided for me by the media from which I could take heart. And I was expected to systematically deprive myself of food just so that I could fit into the image that men want.

'I got talking to Martha, and found out that she'd been thinking much along the same lines, and so we decided to form a breakaway group from our main Women's Group to explore it further. That's when the Fat Women's Support Group was founded. Emma joined us slightly later. Martha, do you want to state our aims?'

'Right, One: we listen to and support each other in our efforts to break free of society's expectations. Two: we campaign to promote positive images of fat women. Three: we pester manufacturers to make larger sizes in fashionable clothes, or more generous furniture. Four: we are creating a new vocabulary for talking about fat. Five: we are encouraging celebrities with weight problems to stop trying to control their weight, and come out, and talk about it.'

'Thanks, Martha. You see, Sandra, we see ourselves as political in the widest sense . . .'

Sandra could not suppress a smile at this unintentional pun.

'. . . and we fight for the right for other women who are still slaves to diet sheets to be themselves.'

'But what if you need to lose weight for medical reasons? Or if you choose to be slim?' Sandra felt compelled to ask this.

Emma, the gentlest of the three, replied.

'Even then, hardly anyone who loses a considerable amount of weight on an imposed diet keeps that weight off for ever. Most women who join organizations like Slim-Plicity, for example, put the weight back on a few months later. Under-eating is unnatural. The pendulum swings back.'

Sandra experienced that familiar feeling of being carried away by somebody else's rhetoric, and the delicious feeling of abandon this gave her. And Emma's last point had a profound effect.

'So any weight I would lose on a diet would be temporary?'

'Almost inevitably. Look, Sandra,' said Liz, 'come and see me during the week. I live in a women-only house in Cheetham Hill. Tell me more about yourself and we'll see what contribution you can make. We're in at the start of a revolution!'

'No, it's all right. I'll come to your next meeting anyway.' Sandra was frightened by Liz's overwhelming personality. 'I'm sure I want to join you. And there's not much to say about me, except I'm a committed feminist and I can see that I was wrong thinking about dieting. I can see that we must change society so that there's a place for us too.'

'Absolutely!' thundered Liz. 'We meet here in a fortnight. The location's not ideal, but Emma's cousin works at the bar here, and has arranged it for us free of charge. And the beer's good. I'm going to eat now, probably at the China Palace. Anyone want to share?'

'I'll join you, Liz,' said Martha.

'I can't,' Emma shrugged. 'I've booked a mini-cab for ten and it's nearly that now. And I've got work in the morning.'

'We'll go, then. See you in a fortnight!' Liz strode off with Martha a pace or two behind her. Sandra waited while Emma locked up.

'Do you want to share my cab?'

'No, thanks. I've got my bike outside. I'll be okay. I've got a personal alarm if I'm in trouble.'

'All right, then. I'll see you in a fortnight.'

Sandra ran quickly down the stairs, left the pub, and found her bike still chained to the GIVE WAY sign. Soon she was pedalling furiously along Heyside High Street. Then she had to stop at the traffic lights. She was hopelessly confused. Dieting was a tyranny. But it made you slim. And she wanted to be slim. But she didn't want to be a sex object. And she'd promised Helen. Now she'd promised these women too. Shit!

She'd been in this sort of mess before. She

53

remembered when she'd promised to canvass for both the Alliance and the Labour Party at the last election when she was in the sixth form. And when she'd arranged to go out with two different boys on the same night. And now, the solution was going to have to be the same. She'd do both. She'd diet for a week and support Helen; diet for another week, skip the Slim-Plicity meeting and then join the FWSG. Just like she did her canvassing on two different days. Yes! Then she could be both slim and show solidarity with her oppressed fat sisters. The lights changed to green and, uplifted, she pedalled on.

Outside the Wellington a Vauxhall Cavalier was parked on double yellow lines. Inside this car, in which the radio came on and off like waves on a seashore, was a small, dark man, sitting in the driver's seat. He was in his late twenties or early thirties, and yet already his hair was thinning on top. His features were small, bird-like and his face seemed to droop. It drooped because he had a moustache that pointed downwards, and eyes that looked careworn and wistful. One could imagine, however, that his face could also suddenly light up, gratified. The melancholy that invaded him now did not seem to be his usual state.

But it was becoming more usual. Len did not like to spend too much time alone, because he had to think, and so, given the opportunity he would strike up conversations with his passengers. But just now he was waiting for a passenger from the Wellington, and unwisely he was early, and nothing could force his thoughts from their familiar pattern.

He would carry on working tonight for another hour or so – he'd told control he'd be around until about eleven. But even if he carried on past that his wife would not care; she'd either be out or fast asleep. And he would be relieved. Because his wife had changed. It was all the fault of that damned slimming club, whatever they call it. Judith had changed from a buxom, cuddly brunette to a skeleton covered over with flesh. They never talked any more. She spent her evenings at her health club, and hours at home soaking in the bath as if she intended to dissolve away her fat. She never asked him what he thought about it. And the reason why she never asked him was because she knew what he would say. That he wanted her to stay as she was. He'd tried everything. When he saw her looking thinner he tried to cook her nourishing meals – dumplings, rag puddings, spotted dicks. But she wouldn't touch them. He'd booked tables at posh restaurants in Manchester, and then he had to cancel the reservations. Then he tried silence, and she became silent.

He couldn't make love to her any more. She reminded him of his mother. His mother had hard, red hands, and when she hugged you, you could feel her bones jutting out and bruising you. When she hit you, it hurt. She kept Len in order by hitting him. She believed that a woman bringing up a boy alone had to be hard. His childhood was full of hard edges. And so his adolescent fantasies were full of fleshy women, embracing, cuddling, enveloping. Judith was like that when he married her. But now she was thin. And their sex life was at an end; probably their marriage too. Thank God there were no children. None of this would he tell anyone. His mother would blame herself for his failed marriage, and he didn't talk about his personal life to his mates.

His passenger still had not come. It was already past ten, so he decided to go into the Wellington to pull his fare out – probably some lager lout drinking with his confederates; at least he had the sense to call a cab. He entered the pub and idly looked around him. He quite fancied a pint, but was religious about never drinking and driving. He watched a girl with spiky hair sprint down the stairs and out through the doors. And then his heart stood still.

Coming down the stairs was the most beautiful woman that he had ever seen. Fair wisps of hair framed a delicately pale complexion; she looked gentle, considerate, intelligent. But it was not just her face; it was her body. Through her black sweat-shirt he could see that she was wearing no bra; her breasts swayed gently and freely as she moved; her nipples protruded slightly. Her tight leggings revealed generously swelling thighs; you could lose yourself in her soft, fleshy body. His own slight body yearned towards her. She came nearer to him, and as she left the pub she brushed lightly against him. He tingled. She was irresistible. He turned to watch her. She did not walk further up the road but stood, uncertain, looking at his Cavalier. Could she be . . .?

He sprang out of the pub and accosted her.

'Are you looking for Apple Cars?'

'Yes. Eight Ship Street, Oldham.'

'That's me.' He heard his voice, unusually gruff. Then he thought he would risk it all. 'I'm afraid as I was coming here the springs in the back seat collapsed. You won't be very comfortable. I suggest you sit in the front.'

To his good fortune she acquiesced. He drove off, and tried to concentrate on his next move. But it was hard. Sitting next to her overwhelmed him. He could sense, rather than see, how, when he pulled up sharply, her body would quiver and shudder, and the surface of her breasts would ripple gently. She seemed so composed and assured; pensive, like a Madonna.

Emma could not help stealing a glance at this unusual mini-cab driver. When he came up to her in the street he looked as if he'd seen a ghost. She wondered if he'd popped into the Wellington for a quick drink; perhaps guilt was responsible for his startled expression. She was puzzled and amused by the deference with which he ushered her into the front seat. She felt rather like a queen and had to remind herself that feminists should not enjoy male courtesy, which was one of the more subtle instruments of oppression. He was small, dark, vital. She looked away. She assumed it must be all right to find a man attractive; she did not believe in separatism and reserved herself the right to have relationships with men, as much as Liz and Martha tried to argue her out of it. She'd gone along with them as far as accepting that marriage, especially hers, was of its very nature an unequal union, but she couldn't help still liking men. Especially slight thin men, a bit like this mini-cab driver. She stole another glance.

She'd timed it badly. The car had stopped at traffic lights and he was looking at her too. Both looked straight ahead immediately. The silence continued.

Five minutes later, 'Do you live in Oldham?'

'Yes.'

'With your husband?'

'Yes.'

Len felt as if the bottom had fallen out of everything. That look of interest she had given him at the lights had allowed him to hope. She was married. Nevertheless he decided to press on.

'Children?'

'No. It wouldn't be fair.'

'Why's that?'

'The marriage isn't really working out.'

Emma surprised herself. Fancy saying that to a stranger, and a man. But sometimes it was safer to talk to strangers, and, after an evening changing the world with Liz, Martha and the rest, it was nice to return to the personal note.

It was hard for Len to suppress the joy in his voice as he inquired why this was. Having been a mini-cab driver for some years now, he had picked up basic counselling skills.

'My husband is a male chauvinist pig. Our marriage was doomed from the start. He expects me to be his servant, and to conform to the stereotypes of his parent's generation. But I've read Simone de Beauvoir and Germaine Greer. He also wants me to lose weight.'

(No! thought Len.)

'And I refuse to mould myself into his idea of a perfect female. I'm me, and have the right to make my choices.'

They were nearly in Oldham. Len could feel that

the palms of his hands were damp, and knew that he had to ask the next question.

'Would that include choosing to come out to dinner with me tomorrow?'

'Sorry? I didn't quite . . .'

'I said, would you like to come out for a meal tomorrow. With me.'

'Is this a joke? Are you another of these ass-holes who think fat women are funny? I suppose you think I spend all my time stuffing myself.'

(But she didn't say 'no', thought Len.)

'No. I don't. Actually I like plump women. I like them a lot better than slim women. And I like you. You seem very honest and intelligent, and I don't want you to get out of this car and walk away. I want to see you again.'

By this time the car had reached Ship Street. Emma saw her husband was not yet home. That gave her time to think. It was foolish and dangerous to make a date with a mini-cab driver. But he had not taken advantage of her on the journey. She liked him. Very confusing. What if she took the initiative now?

'All right. I'm sorry I spoke as I did. I think you might be telling the truth. What's your name?'

'Len Pearce. Number 56/13.'

'Okay, Len. I'll be honest. It does appeal to me, going out with you, but I'm not certain. Can I ring you? Can I contact you at your mini-cab firm? I won't make you wait long; only a few days.'

'If that's how you want it. Please do ring. I do want to see you again.'

Emma felt happy; happier than she had felt for some

months. She took her fare from her purse. Len refused it. She realized it was no use trying to insist. She squeezed out of the cab.

'Bye, Len.'

Len stayed in the cab and watched the voluptuous Emma Hirst let herself in through her front door.

Maureen could not sleep. First she tried lying on her back but it was no good. Then she tried her side, facing away from Joe, and saw from the alarm clock that it was 11.45. It was still Thursday. She turned again but still could not get comfortable. Perhaps if she had something to eat . . .

It was then that she remembered. When she got back from Slim-Plicity she'd defrosted a chocolate gâteau that she was saving for a special occasion. She rang Angie up to come and join her but Phil was at the Boot and she couldn't leave the kids. So there was only her and Joe to share it. Even they couldn't manage the last slice. It was quite a big slice too. A Black Forest gâteau. So Maureen had virtuously thrown it into the bin so that she wouldn't be tempted on Friday when she was going to get into gear. Joe was impressed.

Maureen wasn't normally what you would call an imaginative woman. But lying there in bed she could almost identify with that poor piece of cake, lying in the dark in a nasty, smelly bin, alongside potato peelings and cigarette ash. It was a waste of money too. She never told Joe how much it cost. Her mother would turn in her grave if she knew that Maureen had actually thrown it away.

Very quietly, so as not to disturb Joe, Maureen eased herself out of bed (the springs creaked) and tiptoed across the bedroom. She padded downstairs and went into the kitchen, turning on the light as she did so. She took the lid off the swing-top bin and peered inside. In fact there was only some damp kitchen towel on top of it; the tea-bag had missed it. Perhaps there was some ash on the side.

She picked the cake out of the bin, gave it a quick scrape and ate it, just as Friday began.

CHAPTER FOUR

At two o'clock on Saturday afternoon Helen's phone had rung. It was Tony. The emergency repair he was doing for a firm in Stockport was proving more complicated than he had imagined, and so he wouldn't be home until six or so. This was the problem with having a self-employed husband. Basically they were unreliable. No, that wasn't fair. Tony had to finish the job; he was being paid particularly well, and he did understand that it was going to be a nuisance for her. They had planned that Tony would look after the kids while Helen went to Sainsbury's, a chore that was doubly tiresome when two boisterous children danced in attendance. But it couldn't be helped this week. The trip could not be postponed, as Helen needed fruit and vegetables for herself, and there were sandwiches to think about for Monday as well.

She did not realize she was hungry until she walked through the automatic doors. And even then she wasn't properly conscious of hunger; it was just that the fruit and vegetables looked so much more appetizing than she could remember. The Golden Delicious looked plump and crisp; halves of succulent pineapples were wrapped in cellophane; there were half-pound packets of monkey nuts.

'Matthew! Don't swing on the trolley. You'll tip it over.'

Virtuously she lined the bottom of her trolley with

green mesh bags of Brussels sprouts, leafy cauliflowers, a firm white cabbage and (this was rather extravagant) a quarter pound of mange-tout peas. Now for the salad.

'Matthew! Come back where I can see you.'

Yes; cherry tomatoes – they're that little bit sweeter. Gradually the trolley filled up. Helen felt certain that should anyone glance in her trolley they would be impressed by the commitment to healthy eating that was evident therein.

'Mummy, can I have some sweeties?'

Katy drew her attention to the pick 'n' mix selection in the beginning of the next aisle. To Helen the whole display seemed to exude an aura of sin. The caramel crèmes leered at her. The purple blackcurrant and liquor-ice hinted at unmentionable dark satisfactions. Then the whited sepulchres of mint creams . . .

'No! You'll not eat your dinner. And they're bad for your teeth. You know what the dentist said.'

Cottage cheese. This was an Amber One; eight ounces into the trolley. Edam rather than Cheddar. Shape low-fat cheese spread. (That looks nice.) Now Helen was conscious of her hunger. The sight of food had stimulated her, and she felt quite empty and weak. The hunger actually hurt. She looked with longing at the tempting array of foreign cheese and resolutely pushed the trolley on.

'Mummy! Matthew hurt me. He hurted my leg.'

'Mummy! She's kicked me. You're a poo, Katy.'

'Mummy! Matthew called me a poo.'

'Stop it! You're being very naughty both of you. No crisps if you don't shut up!'

63

Next were the tins. Noodle Doodles, Alphabetti, low-sugar baked beans, baked beans with sausages, tuna in brine. Helen's hunger subsided. Canned food disturbed her senses less.

'This is boring. I want to ride my bike in the park. Daddy said he would take us and it's not fair.'

'I know, Matthew. I'm sure he'll take you tomorrow.'

'No he won't. I'm running away.'

'Come back at once!'

Leaving Katy sitting in state on the half-full trolley, Helen chased her son through several aisles and dragged him back to the trolley, itching to smack him but shy of doing so in public. She could feel herself clenching her teeth. Matthew began to cry. They had reached the fresh meat.

'Look Matthew, if you're very careful not to get lost you can go to the crisps section, and get a packet of crisps for you and Katy. Don't be too long.'

The word 'crisps' electrified Helen as she spoke it. Strange . . . she didn't really like crisps, and yet nothing at the moment seemed so desirable. Crisps. Low-fat ground beef (Amber Ones), bacon and sausages for the kids only, and now for the desserts. Matthew returned clutching the crisps. She thought she would feel jealousy, but instead she experienced a vicarious pleasure at her children's enjoyment of the crisps. Maybe she would let them have chocolate biscuits too. What was she having for dinner tonight? Grilled plaice, Brussels sprouts, cabbage. Oh, well.

Bubble bath, hair shampoo, toilet rolls, kitchen towels, Persil Automatic, Comfort, Coco Pops . . .

'I want to get the Coco Pops!'

'No, me. You're in the trolley.'

'Mummy, I want to get out of the trolley.'

'No! You've got to stay there.'

Helen was aware of a mounting irritation. As she reached the end of the cereal aisle she ground to a halt. Two women with trolleys had stopped to chat, and an assistant unloading muesli made it impossible for anyone to get through. Helen experienced a rapid fantasy of pushing her trolley violently into the woman blocking her way but controlled herself, just murmuring 'excuse me' between clenched teeth.

And then she came to the biscuits. She wouldn't get any for herself, just Tony and the children. She was very hungry. The Chocolate Hob-nobs felt sorry for her. The bourbons were fringed with sadness. She chose Mr Men biscuits, Jammy Dodgers and the obligatory six-packs of Penguins.

'Mummy, Mummy. Can I have a Penguin?'

'Yes, all right. Have you finished your crisps already?'

'No. I not wanted them. I putted them on the floor.'

'Katy! Now how am I going to pay for them? You silly girl!'

'Waah!'

'Now stop it! Here's your Penguin. Where's Matthew?'

Her son was out of her line of vision, just behind her, muttering something about Skeletor. Helen had reached a point of crisis. She was about to enter her own Scylla and Charybdis – in front of her, on the left, were the crisps, Twiglets, peanuts, garlic *croûtons*, honey-roasted cashews. On her right, row upon row of boiled sweets, cellophane packets of fun-size Mars bars. In the past this and the delicatessen were the highlights of her trips to Sainsbury's, the part that made it all worth while. She would choose for herself a number of treats, rewards, indulgences – things for her, not the children, not Tony. Food she could eat alone, in quiet moments. Toffees she could chew while reading a magazine. And all of those were Red. Forbidden. She felt like a small child again, excluded from a game. What if she . . .

With a decision she pushed at the trolley and decided not to even attempt to queue at the delicatessen; she would get the cooked meat she needed from the chilled display instead. Life felt very, very thin. She was tired. She was hungry.

'Mummy! I need a toilet.'

'Didn't you go before we left?'

'No. Matthew was on the toilet.'

At an increased pace Helen filled the rest of the trolley with bread, diet cola, fruit juice, fish fingers and paused to look longingly at the frozen meals for slimmers. They were rather expensive, but surely just one . . . Frozen green beans, four cans of lager for Tony . . .

'Mummy! My wee-wee's coming out.'

'Stop it, Katy!' said Helen violently. 'You know there's not a toilet here and there's nothing we can do. You're a big girl now and you can wait.'

Helen felt like hitting her and was shocked by her own reaction. With increased tenderness she spoke again.

'Look, darling, we're at the check-out now and we won't be long. Why don't you help me unload the shopping?'

Katy twisted round and put single items with great care on to the conveyor belt. Helen mechanically assisted her. Her legs felt quite weak and she wanted something to eat. A sandwich, a huge double decker sandwich. Fish and chips. A cheese and onion pie. Stop it! I'm sure Sandra isn't being as weak-willed as you, she berated herself.

She moved to the other end and put the shopping into the thin plastic carriers provided. They were infernally difficult to open. She rubbed her finger and thumb repeatedly along the top of the bag with little positive result. But rather than irritation, she was flooded with despair. Matthew picked one up and separated the two sides with ease.

'Thank you. You are a good boy.'

'Sixty-seven forty-two, please.'

This was adding insult to injury. Despite the fact she had actually avoided buying herself her habitual treats, her weekly bill was more than average, without counting the subscription and fees for Slim-Plicity. Well, if it has cost this much so far she'd have to stick with it. But it wasn't fair! She was so tired, so drained and so in need of something creamy and sugary and comforting. Or something alcoholic. But she'd committed herself to this uncompromising Spartan regime. She opened the car boot with dull resignation.

Later that evening, when the children were in bed, Tony suggested a take-away. Often on a Friday or Saturday they would share a Chinese, Indian or kebab.

'You get one for yourself, Tone. I'm not really hungry,' said Helen, with very little truth.

On his return from the China Palace, Helen realized that she could not stay in the same room as her husband and watch him eat sweet and sour pork. She went to the kitchen to tidy round. And there on the work surface was a large paper bag containing prawn crackers. They still bore that blush of warmth from the restaurant. Helen was immobilized. Tony would not notice if she had one ... or two. She yearned towards them. And she knew that if she had one she would have another, and another, and possibly send the ever good-natured Tony back to the Palace for more. It would mean the end of her diet. Or she could leave the kitchen, sit in the bedroom, and think about the weight she would lose. Meanwhile the prawn crackers were getting colder ...

Stella awoke with a start. Something was badly wrong. Her breathing was rapid and her stomach felt tender and slightly sore. No light broke through the lined curtains and her bedside clock revealed that it was only 2.30 a.m. An icy sensation travelled along her spine; her head was hot. With an effort of will she remembered ...

Last night Richard had insisted that since it was Saturday, and he was not unduly tired, they should go out to eat. Stella was unenthusiastic: there was still that extra two pounds that needed whittling away. Yet she could hardly parade this as an excuse. He took her to his favourite Italian restaurant. She read the menu with a sinking heart: all of it was rich, all of it was fattening. She ordered the consommé and Richard asked her to share a pizza with him. She agreed. It was delicious. She only meant to have a little, and let Richard have the lion's share, but she didn't. She had all her share. He suggested a dessert. She ordered some cheesecake. And the old madness was back on her. She had cream in her coffee, she had a liqueur. She reached home, and she opened a box of chocolates that was left over from her birthday. She had some more wine. Alcohol helped her fall asleep quickly, which was a boon, but often she would wake for a time in the night.

Wake to the consciousness of a stomach tingling from over-indulgence and the terrifying memory of her binge. How could she have eaten those chocolates too? How many did she have? The strawberry crème, the caramel, the coffee crème (a hundred calories, at least), the nougat, the fudge. And the cheesecake, the liqueur, the pizza. She played them backwards and forwards in her mind like notes on a piano. Her hatred, her contempt for herself knew no bounds. It was impossible to go on living. With her thumb and forefinger she pinched her arm really hard, until she flinched with the pain. That serves you right, you pig. You fat pig. A tear rolled down her face.

She got up to go to the bathroom. Just under the sink were the scales. She put on the light and stood on them, rubbing her eyes so that she could see with absolute precision her exact weight. Nine stone three. Oh, God! She stepped off the scales, waited, and stepped on them again. Nine stone three, or did the needle, for a moment, waver just below the three pounds mark? She stepped off again, moved the scales a fraction to the right where the carpet was thinner. No, it was nine three. One more try. She rested one arm on the sink and put her weight on it. This time the scales registered eight stone ten. But she knew she was cheating. Slowly she removed her arm. Nine stone three. Perhaps if she waited until the morning, the excess food would be digested. Her stomach felt round, like a football. Whatever the scales said, it was back into first gear tomorrow. She had arranged to have lunch with Anne on Tuesday and she must look and feel thin. She returned to bed, awash with guilt. But as she gradually relaxed, she tried to imagine she could hear Jo's voice telling her that no one is perfect, that it's possible to pull oneself back to the straight and narrow, that she was on her side, that she was her friend. Stella slept.

Maureen woke, and decided that if she wasn't going to have a decent Sunday lunch, then neither would anyone else. She'd been in first gear now for two whole days and she'd stuck to it, more or less. Last night in the Wellington she'd kept on the Slimline tonics, and watched everyone get pie-eyed around her. They made right fools of themselves. Everyone was on at her to have just one, and said she was a misery but she wasn't having any of that. She'd show them. Time for her All-Bran now. Joe called them her worms. Today she was cooking dinner for five of them, herself, Joe, Chris and Lisa, and Sharon. She'd already planned the meal, and it gave her some satisfaction.

'D'you need any help, Mum?'

'I'm nearly done now, Sharon, but if you wouldn't mind carrying in some things.'

The joint was already on the dining-room table, cooling now and ready to be carved. Joe regarded it with vast anticipation and inwardly confessed to being somewhat puzzled. Normally when Maureen was dieting Sunday dinners were consigned to the scrap-heap; he remembered the time she served him a cottage cheese sandwich. Perhaps the appearance of the joint heralded the end of this attempt to lose weight. A shame, as he had taken the necessary precautions. He watched his younger daughter bring in dish after dish of steaming food. Strange.

Maureen came in from the kitchen, removing her apron, and throwing it over the back of her chair. She took her place at the table.

'Help yourselves, loves.'

Joe removed the covers from the dishes. Cabbage. Red cabbage. Cauliflower. Brussels sprouts.

'Ee, love, that's nice. What about the potatoes?'

'Not today, we're dieting. No potatoes, no pudding, no gravy. Full of fat, the lot of them.'

Maureen took a pair of white kitchen scales from the sideboard behind her.

'I want exactly three ounces of that beef, Joe, no more and no less.'

Joe carved two slices from the joint and placed them on the scales. They weighed exactly three ounces. He laid them carefully on his wife's plate, and began to carve again.

'And mind Joe, we're all to have three ounces apiece. It's quite sufficient. So you can just check in the scales as you carve.'

She glared around the table, and one by one Chris, Lisa, Sharon and Joe bowed their heads.

'Now I'll help myself to vegetables. They're greens, so they're unlimited.' Her tone of voice was only faintly conciliatory.

Usually the Evans's meals were noisy affairs. This one was funereal. The cabbage was overcooked and watery. Even Maureen left some vegetables on her plate.

'Chris and I will do the dishes, love,' Joe suggested, as one by one knives and forks came to a rest.

'Yeah!' returned Chris, with a shade too much eagerness. Maureen looked at them swiftly surprised.

'It must be so hard for you, Mrs Evans, cooking dinner for us all when you're dieting. You just sit there and me and Sharon will take in the dishes,' Lisa added.

Maureen sat there, dejected and uncomfortable. Too many vegetables always made her feel bloated and windy, and moreover she did not like the menfolk and that Lisa who was living with Chris in her kitchen . . .

'What have you brought?'

'It's all in the Woolworth's carrier.'

Joe opened the Tupperware lunch box to find a large slab of veal and egg pie. He picked it up in his hands and bit into it with relish.

'Steady on, Dad!'

Lisa was still bringing out containers and opening them. The beef and mustard sandwiches were good, if a bit hot. Chris had the cheese and onion pie cold. The carrier had not yet yielded up all its provisions. Lisa had been generous with the emergency supplies. She was a good lass, thought Joe, with gratitude. The four heard footsteps. With commendable rapidity they threw the uneaten food into the bag, and kicked it to one side. By the time Maureen came into the kitchen Joe was up to his elbows in soapy water.

The men were watching the motorcycling. Lisa had gone upstairs with Sharon to look at her new blouse. Maureen was bored and flatulent. She thought she'd better leave the men to it and went into the kitchen to check her family had done a good job with the dishes. Surprisingly it was quite tidy. She was unwillingly impressed. She picked up the carrier bag by the cooker to put it in the pantry where she kept them all. It felt rather heavy. She peered inside. There were empty Tupperware boxes. They smelt good. Maureen was puzzled. They must be Lisa's. Why bring them? She investigated further, and brought out a pound slab of Galaxy chocolate, and a Mr Kipling Manor House cake.

Time stood still. Had Lisa brought them round to tempt her with? Was she going to bring them out later to get her to go off her diet? Typical of that girl! Maureen's mouth watered. They couldn't possibly be for everyone else and not her. Surely even Lisa wouldn't be that cruel? Would she miss a bit of her chocolate? Maureen's temptation to eat was not born of hunger; she was bloated with cabbage. It was strictly emotional. Somebody had brought some food and not told her why. It was possible it was not meant for her. She was left out. She wasn't part of things. It was dreadful at the pub last night, not drinking. It was the feeling of exclusion she couldn't bear. She fingered the chocolate lovingly . . . .

★

Stella stood behind Anne Sargeant on the escalator rising towards the fourth floor of Debenham's and regarded her tiny waist. Anne was wearing a short grey skirt and a white satin blouse, and was carrying her dog-tooth jacket over her arm. All the better to show off her waist with, thought Stella. Stella held her stomach in. She had been eating very little for the past two days, and she could have sworn the scales were just under nine one this morning. She was exhilarated with hunger. Anne and Stella had planned this lunch date a week ago. The pretence existed that they were friends, and indeed no one at HQ thought they were anything but the best of friends. They had a lot in common. They were of a similar age, both married but childless, both successful and committed group leaders. At Slim-plicity there wasn't such a thing as rivalry or competitiveness because everyone was a buddy. Anne's honest, confiding approach was attractive, seductive even, but Anne always succeeded in confiding matters to Stella that she did not wish to know about.

'Oh, Stella, there's something I must tell you. I can't tell this to everyone, you know, as there are some leaders who are so bitchy. But when I was weighed last week at the weekly briefing I was ten pounds under Bull's-eye. It's the lowest I've been. Eight nine!'

'That's wonderful, Anne. You must be delighted,' breathed Stella, fighting her growing depression. And Stella felt mean. Of course she should feel pleased for Anne.

They reached the restaurant. There were separate serving points for snacks, drinks, hot meals and desserts. Each woman waited for the other to begin. The pause was tangible. Anne moved towards the snacks booth.

'I'm not very hungry, Stella. I shall just have a prawn sandwich – oh, without butter and mayonnaise, please,' she added for the edification of the serving girl.

'The same for me, please,' said Stella, secretly resolving to leave half. They moved over to order their black coffees and soon found a table.

Anne did not begin to eat immediately.

'I think it's just as well that Deborah is leaving soon,' she said, pausing for effect.

'Is she? How do you know?'

'You know how indiscreet they are in the office. I just happened to catch a glimpse of her letter of resignation this morning.'

'So Area Co-ordinator will be up for grabs . . .'

'Are you going to apply?'

'Are you?' countered Stella. A pause. 'And what do you mean by "it's just as well that Deborah is leaving"? I thought you got on well with her.'

'I do. She's one of my best friends, and she can't help the fact that she's so indulgent towards the leaders. But she told me that four of us put weight on last week. I think that we're simply not frightened enough of her.'

'Come on, Anne, that's not fair. She's not responsible for what we eat, and anyway, the true spirit of Slim-Plicity is to support, not to criticize.'

'Do you really think that the women who lose weight at your classes do so because you support them?

75

They're frightened of being seen to put on weight. They think you'll tell them off. Take my Mimi Goldberg at Upper Horton. She's lost four and a half stone. Everyone thought she was wonderful. The night I awarded her the Fifty-pound Certificate she was out for a meal to celebrate. Even though she still had two stone to lose she stopped trying. But she's losing weight again now. And do you know why? Because I shouted at her. I told her that any woman who was two stone overweight would still be considered fat, and that she still was fat. And it worked. I'm realistic, Stella.'

Implying, thought Stella, that I am not. And perhaps it's true that I would never shout at a group member. Stella experienced, as usual, both envy and dislike. She toyed with her prawn sandwich, noticing that Anne hardly touched hers. So, Area Co-ordinator was at last vacant. The only two realistic candidates were herself and Anne. Slim-Plicity always appointed senior management from among its own team. Anne had been a leader five months longer than herself, but their track records were similar. It was very awkward.

'Which of your classes might be in the running for the buffet at the Carlton?' Anne inquired.

'I'm not too optimistic. We have some promising new members at Heyside, but it's impossible to say.'

'I'm sure you'll win it, Stella. You inspire your classes so well. I wish I had your enthusiasm. Mind you, Renie Cohen at Upper Horton is trying to lose weight for her daughter's wedding, and she's invited almost the whole group. All of them want to look "a million dollars", as she says, for the day. So the figures are pretty good for the moment. And we've Yom Kippur coming up – the Jewish Day of Repentance. They all fast for twenty-five hours.'

Stella felt more and more depressed. Anne continued.

'I do hope you win it, Stella. I know how much you admire Jo MacKenzie. I'm not such a one for hero-worship, and a buffet with one's group would be rather grim. Imagine them all watching you to see whether you ate or not!' she laughed as each woman eyed the other's sandwich.

Stella laughed dutifully, but with reluctance.

'Are you having a dessert, Stella? I'm going to be wicked and have a meringue.'

'No, no. I'm not really hungry today.'

Hooray, Stella thought. I've eaten less than Anne, and by about three hundred calories. She watched her go to the sweet counter. I was being just as bitchy as her then, Stella thought. Perhaps we're just as bad as each other. Perhaps these diminishing conversations are both our faults. It's quite possible. She felt soiled. Was she just a naïve hero-worshipper? Was she too soft with her groups? No, she thought with resolution. When I become cynical about the slimming business, then I shall give it up. I'm proud to believe in it all, and I don't want to be like Anne Sargeant. Mind you, it was bad news about Upper Horton. A special occasion unites a group. She watched Anne's meringue crumble as she dug her fork into it.

It was hard for Sandra to break the habit of eating while she read. Then she remembered that she had not yet had her apple. She put aside her copy of *The Way of All Flesh* and took an apple from the brown paper bag on the sideboard. Her hunger sharpened her appreciation of its fresh and delicately acidic flavours. She took a large bite and reflected with satisfaction that it was really quite easy to diet. Especially when someone would praise you for having done so well at the end of the week. She was looking forwardly avidly to Thursday, as she had kept to the eating plan with the fervour of a zealot. Of course, she despised it all.

With a pang of guilt, she recalled yet again that she had still not rung Helen. It was her responsibility, as she did not have a phone in the house, and so Helen could not ring her. But the idea of initiating contact with Helen seemed impossible. She was a real housewife, a mother, over thirty probably, with a real life. It was bound to be an inconvenient time if Sandra rang. And what if Helen had not been able to drive carefully, as the manual stated? Then it might seem as if Sandra were boasting. No. It was altogether too risky. But she would certainly make a point of speaking to her on Thursday. She stood up to throw the apple core in the bin. Forty-eight hours to go.

CHAPTER FIVE

Some hung their heads in shame. Others exchanged quiet words of encouragement. Sandra was transported back to her schooldays, when all the girls in her class had their rubella vaccinations. Then they stood in a straggly line, fearful of what was to come, united by a common reluctance to step forward. Sandra was never particularly worried by injections, and now, oddly enough, she was not worried by being weighed at the end of her first week at Slim-Plicity. She was very aware of the tension shared by all of the women in the queue. She supposed that some, like her, had eaten little and were hoping to lose weight. Yet the sullen expressions of several women led her to imagine that they had transgressed. Sandra couldn't imagine paying to come to Slim-Plicity and not dieting. Yet clearly some women did.

In front of her women were beginning to take off their coats and lay them on nearby chairs. It interested Sandra that the woman in front of her proceeded to take off her cardigan too, revealing a thin cotton sleeveless dress, highly unsuitable for an October evening. It dawned on Sandra that this was a fairly painless way to lose weight. Behind the scales, which greeted would-be slimmers in the form of a metallic grey crucifix, was Stella, looking serious as she spoke intently to a number of shamefaced women.

And then it was Sandra's turn. Expressionlessly

Stella placed the metal pointer at eleven stone ten and rapidly moved it down the scales. It balanced at eleven seven. Three pounds. She had lost three pounds.

'Well done, Sandra! That's a super loss. Did you find it easy?'

'Oh, yes! I felt ever so enthusiastic.'

'That's just the way to go about it. I knew you'd do very well. Now read section five in the manual while you wait.'

Sandra slipped her shoes on again and felt encouraged to move away from the scales so the next slimmer could take her place. It was an assembly line. She felt cheated. She wanted to speak to Stella at length so that she could relive her triumphs of the week; she'd remained sober at Adrian's party, she'd had a cottage cheese salad in the refectory when she'd really wanted the lasagne. It was hard, she thought, and really three pounds wasn't such a lot. But it was something. She hugged the knowledge to herself. It was going to be a lot easier being proud to be fat if you were three pounds slimmer. She took a seat near the front and opened her manual.

When Helen arrived the line of women waiting for the scales' assessment of their performance that week had lengthened and looped itself around the back of the hall. Helen joined the line and glanced along it to find Sandra. She could not see her. As for herself, she did not expect to lose weight. She felt no thinner, just tired and irritable, and wondered why she had bothered at all. She had come alone; Judith said she was only going to get weighed and intended to miss the meeting as she was seeing a friend. Now she was back in the British Legion Helen felt as if hardly any-time had elapsed since the last meeting. She had to try hard to remember what had happened to her in the intervening days. Tony's figures were good this month; he'd been cheerful all week. Katy hadn't wanted Helen to take her away from play group on Friday, as she had settled in so well. Matthew's reading was progress-ing. And then there was that awful Saturday when she had had to drag the kids round Sainsbury's, and that night Tony had left the prawn crackers in the kitchen. She hadn't eaten them. She hardly knew why not.

'That's four pounds off! Good girl!' enthused Stella from behind the scales.

Helen was most taken aback. Four pounds was quite a lot. She was initially bemused, and then slowly the pleasure flowed through her. Perhaps she did feel slim-mer after all. The whole room glowed back at her; women seemed livelier, colours brighter, the talking more cheerful. Then she spotted Sandra and immedi-ately approached her.

Maureen did not look happy. Her jaws were clenched, as if with the effort of not eating. Her eyes were small and hard behind her glasses. She saw in front of her Stella and the scales. But through and beyond the visual reality, she saw a slab of Galaxy chocolate and a Manor House cake. These she had not eaten last Sunday, but neither had Lisa gone home with them. She had put them in the washing-machine. It was ingenious. Lisa could not of course ask for them back, as her treachery would have been revealed. When the family had gone, Maureen had removed them, taken them upstairs, and hidden them behind her shoes at the back of her wardrobe. Nobody would look there. And they had been there ever since. But not for very much longer. Everyone knew that what you ate on a Thursday night wasn't cheating. Maureen was intending to eat it all tonight (before Joe brought home the fish and chips).

'You've lost five pounds! That's splendid, Maureen!'

She smiled with grim satisfaction, and a wave of hunger engulfed her as she concentrated her mind upon the food she had stored at home. She felt smug too, and basked in Stella's admiration.

Stella felt cheerful. Her new slimmers had not let her down. They had lost a total of twelve pounds. And the week's losses seemed encouraging. She was conscious yet again of enjoying her job, and doing it well.

'Hello, Sandra.'

'Helen! Sit down. I'm ever so sorry I didn't phone – I was worried I'd be intruding. Did you have a good week?'

'Average. Doing the usual sort of things.'

'No. I mean a good week dieting. Have you lost any weight?'

'Oh, yes. Four pounds. And you?'

'Just three.'

'But that's very good. That's half a stone between us. Have you found it easy going?'

'Yes. I've been carried away by it, rather. When I get down to it, I don't mind not eating.'

'I'm afraid I do. It's been a miserable week in a way. I've missed the food and I've had to make a conscious effort not to eat. But I'm glad I've lost four pounds.'

'It's worth it, isn't it?' said Sandra, inquiringly.

'To be honest I don't know yet. I've been bad-tempered and depressed, not being able to eat. But the thought of being slim again is very enticing.'

'Do you really think so? I know some women who are proud to be fat. They think they should have the right to be themselves, and not be forced into the strait-jacket of thinness to suit a male-dominated society.'

'But it's the women themselves who want to be slim. I'm not dieting for Tony or any other man. I'm dieting for me.'

There was an uncomfortable pause. Sandra could not think of an answer. Both women listened to the conversation taking place behind them.

'. . . a baked potato in its jacket. But you can always have natural yoghurt instead of butter. If you mix it with low-calorie mayonnaise . . .'

'Yeah, I know, but I've always liked mine dripping with garlic butter with some grated cheese on top. All forbidden.'

'If there's one thing I can't stand about this place it's that everyone talks about food,' whispered Helen. 'Let's talk about something else. Tell me about you. What's it like being a student?'

'What do you mean?'

'What do you do? How do you spend your time?'

'Well, I go to some lectures during the day. I read in the library most afternoons. I'm doing a course on the nineteenth-century novel, and that means a lot of reading. We're starting Dickens next week. I see my friends most evenings, and then there are parties on the weekends, or bands play gigs at the Union. The Stone Roses, bands like that. It's mainly reading and listening and talking, I suppose. Is that what you mean?'

'Is the work hard?'

'Not really. I'm not as good as I'd like to be. My tutors say that my critical analysis is sometimes very woolly. Look. I think Stella's finished weighing now. She'll be starting soon.'

Helen envied Sandra's enthusiasm, and more than that, envied her life. How wonderful to be so free of responsibilities, and to have an education. Still, she wouldn't have missed out on the children. She suddenly resolved to go to the library with Katy tomorrow and this time get a book for herself too. Maybe even something by Dickens!

Sandra felt guilty. She hadn't rung Helen, and now she was planning to skip the next Slim-Plicity meeting too. And she liked Helen. She felt comfortable with her, and was flattered and warmed by her interest. Sandra began to think that age might not be a barrier to friendship. Perhaps she could baby-sit for Helen or something. She probably didn't get out much. Kids must tie you down. She wondered how Helen spent her time . . .

'Good evening, ladies. We've had a great week this week, the first competition week, and the figures look good. And your figures look good too! This week I've also got some recipes for fish dishes and low-calorie desserts. But first the losses . . .'

Judith was worried and tearful. She camouflaged herself in the bus queue and looked at her watch again. It was eight o'clock. She had arranged to meet Geoff early tonight. She had popped into Slim-Plicity just as it had opened, and delighted Stella with her three-pound loss. She was now well and truly under Bull's-eye. Len thought she was staying for the whole meeting and going for a drink with some of the girls later. Her intention, however, was to spend the whole evening with Geoff. He had said that he would pick her up at the same place – across the road from the bus stop – at seven thirty. He was not there. For the first ten minutes she was not particularly worried. Then she began to fret. Had his wife stopped him coming? There was no way she could find out. Or worse still, had he decided not to come – was it all over? That was unthinkable. She felt weak with fear. Or perhaps there had been an accident? He could be dying in intensive care, and she would not know. Somehow this was preferable to him deciding to finish their romance. He had become very, very important to her. She had become slim for him. He was her new life. They would live together, in a smart flat somewhere. And they had not yet made love. She tingled. And then remembered again that he was late. She felt physically sick. With the sound of every approaching car her heart lifted, and then sunk. The sound of an altogether larger vehicle was heard, and a brightly lit bus squealed to a halt at the shelter and disgorged several passengers. Judith rapidly scanned their faces and was relieved to recognize none. The women in the queue boarded the bus, and one young girl – hadn't Judith seen her at a Slim-Plicity meeting? – had trouble getting the ticket machine to accept her Clipper Card. The driver had to leave his booth and assist her. Eventually it was sorted out, and the bus shivered into action. As it moved off it revealed, on the other side of the road, a blue Fiesta, registration number RND 178Y.

'I'm taking you back to my house, Jude.'

'But what about your wife?'

'It's finished. We've had a massive argument. That's why I'm so late.'

'Was it about me?'

'No. She doesn't know about you – yet. But it's something almost as serious.'

'Do you want to talk about it?'

'Yes, Jude. I'll tell you on the way. I want to take you home with me.'

Geoff turned the key in the ignition, and the radio came on automatically. He switched it off. The car gathered speed as the back streets of Heyside flashed by. As Geoff spoke, Judith felt curiously detached from his narrative, as he looked straight ahead at the traffic, occasionally checking the rear-view mirror, and rarely looked at her.

As he talked he did not think of Judith. Instead he relived the hurt and anger, and saw the scene play again in his mind . . .

He had been waiting for Emma to come in for twenty minutes. He had not eaten; he intended to re-proach her with his hunger. No normal woman would neglect her man as Emma had neglected him. The dining-room was small, claustrophobic. The house was meant to be only a temporary stop until their joint in-comes enabled them to buy something rather larger for

the family that had never, and would never material-
ize. This was a poky house, and, as Geoff looked
around, he blamed the whole house on Emma. The
table that he was sitting by, a mahogany gatelegged
table, was smeared with grease and was slightly
scratched. The carpet needed hoovering. The dried
grasses in the fire grate were dusty. A proper wife
would have seen to all these things. A proper wife
would have been satisfied with working part time at
the library, and would not have opted for full-time
work, including evenings. He was dimly conscious of a
miaowing at the french windows leading into the small
garden. He would not feed the cat. That was her job.
Emma was unnatural. Women enjoy feeding animals,
and men. And she refused to start a family. He wanted
a son.

He heard the key turn in the latch, and he knew he
was spoiling for a fight; his muscles were tense with
anger. Emma's bulk filled the doorway.

'I'm home, Geoff.'

'Without an apology?'

'For what?'

'Most wives get in before their husband. Most wives
might think of cooking him a meal.'

'Oh, God – not again.'

'My mother cooked a hot meal for my father every
day. She looked after him. And she looked after herself.
A woman should be proud of her appearance. Look at
you.'

Emma was wearing short trousers of a patterned
cotton fabric. Over these was an extra-large black T-
shirt. Her blonde hair was dishevelled. Geoff compared

her to Judith and found his wife repulsive, a heavy encumbrance.

'Look, Geoff, I've had enough too. You don't want a wife – you want a slave. I think I've made a terrible mistake, marrying you. But I must, for my own sake, give you one more chance. I stayed late at the library to work out a rota. If we can stick to this, and share the jobs in the house fairly, and we agree to talk in the evenings rather than you watching telly every hour God sends, and if you can accept that I want to look the way I do, then there's a chance for us.'

A rota. What was this, the army? Geoff felt violent and only with Herculean effort did he stop himself striking her. A rota. How dare she. Stop watching the box. It was his right. He earned the money to rent that telly. She wasn't normal, couldn't be, wanting to look like that, fat. Look at Judith. She knew what a man liked. She kept herself slim. He felt very sorry for himself but wouldn't acknowledge it. All he was truly conscious of was an overwhelming anger and sense of outrage. She expected him to do all that? A rota.

'Well, Geoff, what do you say? Shall we try again?'

'Fuck off!'

Emma didn't seem to respond. She only said, 'I've given you a chance. You haven't taken it. I'll ring him up now. It's finished, Geoff. I probably won't be home tonight.'

And she walked out. Geoff was furious, he was relieved. How dare she? He'd kill her. But he was free. And he had Judith. He got up and kicked the gate-legged table very hard. It shivered and rocked. His foot throbbed. He picked up his empty coffee mug that was lying on the table and hurled it into the kitchen. It smashed into the dresser and lay on the floor in fragments.

'That stupid bitch.'

He stormed upstairs to get changed and meet Judith.

Judith watched the anger play on his face and thought it made him look really sexy. She thought his wife sounded awful; peculiar, really. Fancy not looking after your husband. Perhaps she was a lesbian or something. A fleeting discomfort invaded Judith, as she made an involuntary association with Emma; Emma had slept with Geoff; Judith intended to. She would not think of her. She dismissed Emma from her mind.

The car stopped in a street of terraced houses, built of Accrington brick. Judith was slightly surprised that her future lover should live somewhere so modest; Geoff Hirst, the international financier, inhabited a smart, masculine penthouse flat, slept in a bed with black sheets, had a bedside telephone-answering machine. The reality was different. The house that Geoff ushered her towards was small and undistinguished. It had a compact front garden with an unkempt, straggly patch of grass. The harsh yellow light from the street lamp opposite revealed that the front door was painted a burgundy red, and that in places the paint was peeling. Judith quickly adjusted her thoughts. Geoff Hirst, the hard-working mill hand, unfairly dismissed by his penny-pinching employer, opened his humble front door and entered the dark, narrow corridor. He switched on the electric light and Judith noticed the 'dolly mixtures' patterned wallpaper (rather dated) and trod on the local free newspaper which had been recently delivered. The interior of the house seemed cramped. In front of them was the entrance to one room; on the right was a door which led into a small, square lounge. Next to this door was an uncarpeted flight of stairs.

Geoff led Judith into the room facing them; he switched on a large standard lamp with a dusty red shade. It partly illuminated the room. Ahead of Judith were some french windows; in front of these was a gatelegged mahogany table, which looked as if it had seen better days. The square Indian-style carpet was slightly threadbare. Judith wondered why they didn't have a fitted carpet; everyone she knew did.

Geoff took her in his arms.

'Judith . . .'

She loved his embrace. But she was disorientated. As he kissed her hungrily she noticed that the undrawn curtains were partly coming away from the rail. She had an urge to go and see to them. Geoff was rhythmically rubbing her back. Still she could not close her eyes. She saw a cat slink along the wall in the back garden, and it wailed. She was not relaxed and she had to stop him. She pulled away slightly.

'It's no good. I'm not ready yet. Have you got a drink or something?'

'Sure. That's a good idea.'

Geoff kissed her on the forehead and turned on the light in the kitchen. She heard the fridge open, and he came back with two cans of Hofmeister lager. Judith was horrified. She couldn't possibly drink that: it was nearly two hundred calories a can. And yet she had never felt so badly in need of a drink.

'Do you have anything else?'

Geoff thought for a moment. 'There might be some brandy left over from Christmas.'

Soon Judith was sitting on the edge of a moquette armchair, holding a small glass of brandy (about fifty calories). Geoff muttered something, and went back into the kitchen. While he was gone, Judith held her nose and quickly gulped down the contents of the glass she was holding. Geoff was gone rather a long time. When she heard the distant sound of a chain pulling she realized that there must be a toilet through the kitchen. Not very hygienic, she thought. Again she was aware of a faint distaste. Even her ready stream of fantasies was drying up. She sat very still and was aware of the heat of the brandy.

Geoff stood at the door of the kitchen, drying his hands on a tea-towel.

'Feeling better?' he inquired.

'Mmm.'

'Coming upstairs?'

Judith thought she had better go to the bathroom first. Geoff explained that the only bathroom they had was an extension built on to the kitchen. He would wait for her in the dining-room. As she stood he embraced her once again; she could feel his readiness for her. That was exciting. She broke away again and went into the kitchen.

There were dirty bowls near the sink that looked as if they had contained cornflakes, or muesli. On the quarry-tiled floor was a broken coffee mug. There was a smell of sour milk. Judith could not resist opening the cupboard opposite the sink. On the door was a stark poster which read 'Women constitute half the world's population, perform nearly two thirds of its work hours, receive one tenth of the world's income and own less than one hundredth of the world's property'. Judith read it without the sense sinking in. Inside the pantry was a large carrot cake, some boxes of cereal, tins of cat food, beans and soup, and three bulging packets of Bombay mix. Judith shut the door and went into the bathroom.

The pale blue toilet seat was loose, and when she sat on it, it shifted to the right and her flesh was momentarily shocked by contact with the cold porcelain. Opposite her on a shelf were the various soaps, talcs and lotions that Geoff and Emma used. She washed her hands at the sink, and noticed some fair hair clogging up the plug hole. Geoff's? Emma's? In the bath was a clothes-horse, with some underwear hanging on it. Look at the size of those knickers! Judith checked the label. XXL. She felt as smugly horrified as a small child in an infant classroom might, seeing her friend, not her, spoil a picture by colouring out of the lines. On a lower rung were Geoff's Y-fronts. They had holes in them. His socks, too, needed heeling. There was no clean towel in the bathroom and Judith shook her hands dry. She could not summon up one fantasy. She had never felt less like sex in her life.

Geoff was just finishing his lager when Judith returned.

'My period's just started,' she lied. Geoff stood there wordlessly and she felt sorry for him.

'Look,' she said, 'I want our relationship to start off somewhere quite new. Not here. Your wife lives here.

Can't we go away together? I can easily lie to Len, and, from what you've told me, your wife won't mind. Can we?'

'Well, I don't see why not. Where were you thinking of?'

'Not too far. Somewhere in the country. A small hotel. Can you find somewhere?'

Geoff was gratified. At least she asked him to arrange it all. And it was a good idea; it certainly appealed to him. A real dirty weekend.

'Leave it to me. I'll make a booking and I can pop into your office to give you the details.'

The receptionist at Raffles Hotel, Singapore, smiled knowingly at the couple who had booked themselves in as Mr and Mrs Geoffrey Smith. The bell boy took their leather suitcases into the lift . . .

It was a little after half past nine, and Judith suggested that they go elsewhere for another drink before the end of the evening. She retrieved her fake-fur jacket from behind the armchair and both of them prepared to depart. Judith left first, and stood by the gate while Geoff locked the front door. His Fiesta was parked in front of the house, part of a more or less contintious line of cars along the street. Obviously the convention was for cars to park on this side, as the road was too narrow to allow parking on both sides. Judith listened idly to an approaching car engine. A Vauxhall Cavalier drove slowly along the road, and clearly intended to park just behind Geoff. Geoff walked down the short garden path, put his arm round Judith's waist, and ushered her through the gate. That was when she recognized the car as Len's. She felt very sick, as the adrenalin surged through her body.

'Quickly, Geoff. Get into the car quick. Quick!'

Geoff opened the passenger door and she slid in. He too entered rapidly and soon the car moved off. Judith's heart was beating fast. Was Len spying on her? Or was this just an awful coincidence, him taking a fare that lived in Geoff's street? In her panic she had not seen the woman in the front seat of the cab . . .

But the woman had seen her. Emma had seen a slim brunette standing by her gate, and she had seen her husband drive off with her. He doesn't waste any time, she thought. But then, neither did I.

'That was my husband, Len. Looks like he's got another woman.'

Len was quite unaware of this drama. He had been concentrating on the distance between the Fiesta and the Metro a little way behind, preparatory to manoeuvring into the only vacant parking space in the street. Once Emma had spoken, all he could see were the disappearing tail lights of the Fiesta. Len parked the car.

'Do you mind? You've told me it was all over.'

'To think that I insisted we come back here because I was worried about that shit. I was actually worried about him.'

'You don't have to think about him now. Do you want to go back and have another pint?'

Emma burst into tears.

'Oh, God. This is so silly. I don't even like him any more. But it's the speed. I only walked out on him two hours ago. And I waited all week to ring you up. And I wouldn't have if he hadn't sworn at me.'

'I want you, Emma. You know that.'

'Yes, I do. I think I want you too. It was very important to me, that conversation we had tonight. Let's talk some more.'

'Where? Back to the pub? Or do you want us to go into your place?'

'I want to be alone with you, but not in that house. I never want to set foot in it again. Let me think.'

Len took a tissue from the box in the glove compartment and wiped away her tears. Emma began to smile. She opened her handbag and brought out a set of keys.

'They're Liz Breen's. I'm looking after them for her while she's away on a women-only rock-climbing course on Ilkley Moor. She knew I was having trouble with Geoff and said I could use her room as a sanctuary. We'll go there!'

Len turned the key in the ignition.

'Oh, no. I've just remembered. It's a woman-only house. They won't let you in . . . Never mind. We'll think of something . . .'

The Cavalier coasted slowly along a row of imposing semi-detached Victorian dwellings, part of an abrupt cul-de-sac that ended in a mass of untrimmed hedgerows. The car came to a rest at the end of the street, and all the lights were turned off. A large, dark figure emerged and made her way carefully to the last house on the row. She ascended the few steps to the front door, opened it, and was swallowed up by light and noise.

All was silent in the street below. Fifteen minutes later the woman reappeared from the alley by the side of the house. She revisited the Cavalier and brought forth from it a small, slight figure in a dark leather jacket. Swiftly she led him back along the side of the house and into the back garden.

The garden was almost entirely dark, and Len was only dimly aware of the greyish masses that must be trees. Emma brought him up a short flight of stone steps to an unlit kitchen. It felt like a children's game; hide and seek, or blind-man's buff. Len was enjoying himself very much. Holding him by the hand, Emma led him along the kitchen and pointed silently to a flight of stairs. Both ascended in absolute silence. As they turned the corner in the stairs they heard voices.

'Quick!' whispered Emma. She moved swiftly up the rest of the stairs, and opened a door, and motioned Len to come inside. She shut it behind them. They stood locked in an embrace compounded of fear, laughter and a deepening excitement.

Len looked quickly around. The room they were in was more like an office than a bedroom, decorated with political posters, and containing as its centre-piece a large deal table covered with sheaves of paper. But at the front of his awareness was Emma, at last. He had been obsessed with her all week. Waking at night, he had tried to conjure up her image which had remained enticingly elusive. And then she had called him, and here she was.

It was better than he had imagined. As they lay on the bed and kissed slowly he became aware of the wealth of pleasure she could offer. Once he had stayed at a cousin's house at Christmas. And the dining-table there was heavily laden with food. Len remembered and re-experienced that tremulous anticipation. They removed their clothes. Len was lost in the profusion of softness and warmth enveloping him. Her flesh was like silk, with a fluid, melting quality. He buried his head in her breasts. Once again he was a baby. And then, as she gained confidence and ran her hands over him, exploring him, he was overcome with a new, powerful desire for her. Yet he held back as he made acquaintance with every part of her soft, generous body. Her rapid breathing excited him further. He was lost, and reborn, inside her.

CHAPTER SIX

'Heyside 776038?'

'Hello. Can I speak to Helen, please?'

'It's me. Be quiet, Katy!'

'It's Sandra. How are you?'

'Okay. And you?'

'All right. How's your diet going?'

'Well, I think. Katy! Get off the window-sill – you'll fall.'

'Am I ringing at a bad time?'

'No, it's always like this. How are you getting on with the diet?'

'Okay. But there's something I feel guilty about. That's why I'm ringing.'

'Wait a minute. Katy's hurt herself. I can't hear for the crying.'

'Hello. Helen?'

'I'm back again. Go on, Sandra.'

'I can't make the meeting on Thursday. Well, I'm going to get weighed, but that's all. I want to talk to you about it.'

'Stop crying! Look, Sandra, can you come round. It's much easier.'

'Can I?'

'Please. You're only in Middleton, aren't you?'

'Yes. When shall I come?'

'Not now. It's after *Playbox*. Sorry. I mean, why not this evening? Tony's working late again. Come over about six.'

Sandra eased herself into the armchair by the gas fire, and sat on a small, hard object that later revealed itself to be a metallic blue tractor. In the armchair opposite was a fair, pretty child dressed in Postman Pat pyjamas. She smiled at Sandra with shy interest. Unused to the company of small children, Sandra felt hesitant about striking up a conversation. Does one talk to a small child as if she is an adult? Or do you just ask them a series of questions? Katy smiled on.

In the kitchen, pouring hot water from the kettle into two coffee mugs, Helen too felt uncertain. To her Sandra represented another way of life distinct from hers, and very desirable. That Sandra was young did not matter; Helen always felt that she herself had never grown up past twenty. It was just that, by inviting a student to her house, she knew she had done something out of the ordinary. It was an unfamiliar, and rather exciting, feeling. Biscuits? Perhaps not. She gave each mug a quick stir, and carried them into the lounge.

'Can I sit on your lap?'

'If you like,' said Sandra, rather flattered by this direct approach. The child perched on her knees and looked up at her reverently.

'Why have you got sticky-up hair?'

'Katy! Don't be so rude. Go and play in the bedroom with Matthew,' Helen commanded, flushing with embarrassment.

'Oh, it doesn't matter! I like children!' said Sandra, as if she were discovering the fact for the first time. 'I put gel on it.'

'Jelly?'

'Hair gel.'

'Here we are.' Helen produced some paper and felt-tips from a drawer in the sideboard. 'Draw Sandra a picture.'

Sandra wondered when she and Helen would get a chance to talk. She had not realized how intrusive small children could be. Of course, she had no real experience of any. But soon Katy became absorbed in her picture, and Helen was smiling at her encouragingly.

'Right. As I said on the phone, I'm not staying for the meeting on Thursday. I'm going somewhere else. You see, in the Wellington there's a meeting . . . well, some women . . . the Fat Women's Support Group. Sorry, I'm not making myself clear. I also want to join this Fat Women's Support Group. It meets on the same night as Slim-Plicity. I think I mentioned them to you. They're the women who believe that it's okay to be fat. They're proud of it,' said Sandra, shamefully.

'Aren't you going to Slim-Plicity any more?' asked Helen with real disappointment.

'I might. I don't know. It's just that I can see their point too. Why go through the agonies of dieting purely to be the shape that society demands you should be? It's artificial.'

'I suppose you could see it like that.'

'As a feminist I can't see why I should suffer just to make myself into the acceptable stereotype for the moment. In other cultures fat women are considered beautiful, even sexy. I think by belonging to Slim-Plicity you collude in the oppression of women, and their right to be individuals.'

'But the women who go to Slim-Plicity choose to go there of their own accord. It's not as if they're taken in a chain-gang by their husbands.'

Sandra laughed, confident in being able to knock down this familiar argument.

'Conditioning. Over the centuries Western women have been taught that unless they learn how to please men, there is no place for them. It's become so deeply ingrained that we have internalized men's expectations of us. We now condition ourselves to fit the acceptable stereotype. It's hard to break this pattern – harder than a simple act of rebellion against an external tyrant – but women owe it to themselves and their sisters to do so. And think what you can eat if you're not always on a diet!'

'But I know I looked nicer when I was slimmer.'

'Not in absolute terms. And why judge someone just by the proportion of flesh to bone? Look at you now. You've got a family that loves you, and you're friendly, and intelligent, and so helpful to talk to. You wouldn't be any better if you were slim. And you might not be any happier. I lost a stone and a half when I was sixteen. I spent all that summer looking in the mirror examining myself in case I got fat again, and dreading the next time I would be tempted to eat something I shouldn't.'

'That's not right.'

'But that's what happens. Women suffer from anorexia through obsession with slimming. Some women make themselves throw up every day so they won't put weight on. Is that desirable?'

Helen was beginning to feel the effects of Sandra's

fierce rhetoric. Little of it related to her experience, but she was flattered by Sandra's estimation of her. She was surprised too at her disappointment that her new and very different friend would be leaving Slim-Plicity. She must make a direct appeal.

'I can see that it's easy to become addicted to slimming, like anything else, but I don't think I am. Yet. Please don't leave Slim-Plicity.'

'I'm not leaving,' said Sandra hastily, unable to let anyone down, 'it's just that I also want to go to the Fat Women's Support Group – sometimes. I don't suppose I've really convinced myself yet that it's okay to stop dieting. What do you think of Slim-Plicity, Helen?'

'It offers me hope. Stella is so optimistic. And dieting isn't always bad. There are times when it's really painful not to eat, but then, at other times, you feel proud of yourself for not being so dependent on food. What I find funny, though, is the way that everyone at meetings talks about food all the time. You'd think they'd want to forget about all the things you can't eat.'

'Right!' exclaimed Sandra, enthusiastically. 'And doesn't everybody look miserable. And so ashamed when they've put weight on. Like sinners at confession!'

Helen laughed.

'It is. It's like the twentieth-century religion! We worship slim women. To overeat is to transgress. Every week we make a pilgrimage to the scales to be judged. Stella preaches at us. Food, like the devil, tempts us. Thinness is the new orthodoxy of our time. Wow!'

Helen shared Sandra's pleasure at her own discovery.

'And there is a connection,' Sandra continued rapidly. 'Lots of actual religions use fasting as a way of inducing religious feeling. Not eating creates a sort of light-headedness, a euphoria. And also some religions have loads of food laws – you can't eat pork, you can't eat cows, and people are so busy working out what they can and can't eat they simply don't have time to question the orthodoxy. You'll never catch Stella at a Slim-Plicity meeting exploring why it's worth dieting. It's accepted unquestioningly. But should it be?' she concluded triumphantly, flushing with pleasure.

Helen was left with an impression of Sandra's enthusiastic intelligence and powers of argument. She was uneasy too. Perhaps there was something in what she was saying. She hadn't thought about it before. And yet she had her doubts.

'But it's ugly to be fat. And you can't be fat and sexy.'

'These women in the Fat Women's Support Group – they're not all ugly, and anyway, sexuality is a very personal thing. You agree with me really, don't you, Helen?'

'You've got a point. I'll think about it. But if you do end up going to these other meetings, we can still meet up afterwards, can't we? I enjoy talking to you.'

'You mean you enjoy listening to me talk,' said Sandra ruefully. 'But of course we can. I want to.'

'You see. Meeting you was a good thing to come out of Slim-Plicity. And since I haven't been eating all day long, I seem to have had more time to do things.'

'Like what?'

Helen thought hard, and was invaded with a feeling

of discomfort. There was something that had happened that she was trying to forget, and Sandra's innocent question had made her half remember. What was it? Yes. She'd decided to take Katy to the library. It was good for her, and Helen needed to get out of the house. While Katy was looking at the picture-books Helen had recalled Sandra's mention of Dickens. Why not? She moved over to the general fiction section and found a book by Dickens called *The Pickwick Papers* and had taken it out. Later that night, when Tony was watching the European football, she'd opened it, certain that she too was capable of reading a real book. But she wasn't. She couldn't understand a word. No, it wasn't that. She could have understood it if she'd tried hard enough, but the book didn't interest her. It wasn't about anything. And she was kidding herself if she thought that she could read what Sandra was reading. There was an unbridgeable gap.

'Like what?'

'Giving the bedrooms a proper clean. Taking Katy to places – to the library.'

'What do you like reading, Helen?'

'Magazines, mostly.' And then, as if to shame herself further, 'I did try some Dickens this week, but it was much too hard.'

'What did you read?'

'*The Pickwick Papers*.'

'Oh, no! That'll give you completely the wrong idea. I've never been able to get into it myself. You must try something else. Let me think ... Who do you remind me of? Of course! Biddy! Have you read *Great Expectations*, Helen?'

'No.'

'Well, you must. It's probably Dickens's best novel. It's about all sorts of things, but mainly the effect that adults can have on children when they try to mould them to their wishes. Conditioning, I suppose. It's about a little boy called Pip, and in the beginning he gets to go and play at the house of this eccentric old woman – let down by a man, of course . . .'

Sandra made it all sound so easy and interesting.

'. . . and an appalling uncle, who keeps asking him to solve impossible sums. Promise me you'll read it, Helen.'

'All right.'

'And there have been some really good films of it too. Dickens's adaptations are often on telly. And *Little Dorrit*'s recently been released at the cinema. Do you go to the cinema much?'

'No. It's not always easy to get a baby-sitter.'

'I'm not a baby,' complained Katy. She got up from the floor holding a grubby, multi-coloured picture in her hand. She thrust it at Sandra.

'This is for you.'

'Thank you. What is it?'

The three of them became aware of a loud thumping, rapidly coming closer. A small figure burst in through the open doorway and launched himself at the settee, bounced on it once, and did a backward somersault off it on to the floor.

'That's Matthew,' said Helen, unnecessarily.

The fair, tousled boy grinned at Sandra.

'Are you my mummy's friend?'

'Yes.'

'My friend is called Danny. He's in Mrs Hardy's class. Are you a teacher?'

'Sorry about this, Sandra. He'll keep you talking for hours.'

The apology was unnecessary. Sandra was enjoying herself. She had not realized that children were so unquestioningly affectionate and conversational. Then she had an idea.

'Helen. I'd like to baby-sit for you. I'd enjoy it. You need a break from being stuck at home all the time. Please.'

Katy sidled up to her, and stroked the fringes on her skirt.

'Please be my baby-sitter.'

'Can I, Helen?'

Delighted, but innately reluctant to take advantage of anyone, Helen remained silent.

'I wouldn't say it if I didn't want to.'

'Well, all right. Next time we have the chance to go out I'll ask you first.'

Katy hoisted herself on to Sandra's lap and reached up to finger her metallic ear-rings.

'Will I see you at the Slim-Plicity meeting on Thursday, Sandra? Will you go?'

'No, I won't stay for the meeting. But I'd like to see you afterwards. Why don't we have a drink in the Wellington? I could meet you there when we've both finished. Then we could swap notes.'

'That's a good idea. Say about nine o'clock?'

Stella lay flat on her stomach, naked except for a brief pair of pants. Her arms hung down loosely on either side of the narrow wooden table, her head was turned to the right. She breathed deeply to inhale the nutty aroma of the oil that the masseuse was rubbing and pushing into the backs of her calves. Her weekly massage had just begun. As yet Stella was not relaxed, but was enjoying the sensation of receiving attention rather than giving it. The heat of the masseuse's hands glowed through to the muscles of her legs. The feeling of uncomfortable vulnerability that Stella experienced when first coming to Linda, her masseuse, was now replaced by a wary appreciation. She loved being pampered, and yet an odd squeamishness in her rejected the physical pleasure she received. It was strange. Stella tensed her foot as Linda raised it and held it against her stomach to rub the ankles. Stella cursed herself as she remembered that the right thing to do was to let the foot go floppy to show Linda that you were totally relaxed. She could feel Linda's flat stomach against the sole of her foot. She was glad that Linda was slim, as she could not bear to have someone fat touching her. She did not stop to ask why. She felt no jealousy of Linda, who was a close and special friend. And it was particularly pleasant when Linda commented on how well she was keeping her weight down. Stella tensed again as Linda pressed against some very tender muscles.

Yes, she felt no jealousy of Linda. Then perhaps all the sourness and suspicion that existed between her and Anne Sargeant was of Anne's making, not hers. Yet she felt guilty too. What relief when she could unburden herself to Richard and talk about Anne mercilessly. Just now, she felt certain that Anne was campaigning quite openly for the position of Area Co-ordinator. Stella could not bring herself to do that. The job would mean nothing to her unless she was selected fairly. Or perhaps these days you had got to look after number one. Anne had spent hours in the past week closeted in Deborah's office, almost as if Anne were already taking over the job from her. It was clever. Anne seemed to be creating an image for herself of someone who ought to have authority thrust upon them by being almost permanently in the company of the powerful. And she made absolutely sure that Stella was aware of this. She had actually had dinner with the Carters. Michelle Carter would be interviewing for Area Co-ordinator, and Anne's husband worked with John Carter. And Anne is so poised and charming at these social occasions. Stella didn't stand a chance.

Linda covered Stella's legs with a soft woollen towel, warm with the heat from the radiator. She anointed her hands with more aromatic oil and rubbed them along Stella's back. She always enjoyed this part. She became conscious of her body as being composed of bone and muscle, and she felt strong in herself. Usually Stella watched her body with the vigilance of a sentry trained to look out for the enemy, in her case, fat. But Linda's hands drew attention to the life in her body. The smoothing and pressing of her muscles, the heat generated by the whole procedure, made Stella feel as if she were being ironed. And the irony is, thought Stella, that Anne keeps telling me that she thinks I'll get the job. 'You'd make a super Co-ordinator,' she breathed, 'you're so popular.' She is either not certain of her own chances, or she is deliberately trying to make it worse for me when I don't get the job. Stella wished she was not so vulnerable to Anne's praise. Ow! Linda pressed into a tightly knotted muscle. The sudden pain she felt gave vent to a spurt of anger.

It wouldn't be so bad if Anne would make a good Area Co-ordinator. But she's an unprofessional group leader. Stella knew that she behaved contrary to the spirit of Slim-Plicity. For example, there were several cases when her group members failed to score Bull's-eye on the evening they were expected to, and Anne had arranged for them to attend another group's meeting one or two nights later and get weighed again, just so her monthly figures for HQ could look good. Stella had even heard it rumoured that Anne set her scales half a pound below zero on nights when she thought her group might have done badly. But as Linda massaged her spine she stiffened as she remembered a rather more disturbing affair.

She was having coffee with Anne on Friday. Black, no sugar. Anne was laughing about the confessions of one of her slimmers from her Upper Horton group. Apparently this woman was completely off her rocker. She'd begun by asking Anne whether it was all right to save her Amber Twos and Amber Threes until bedtime, as she liked to have some toast and butter before she went to bed. She said she felt very guilty doing this. Anne had to reassure her that it was perfectly all right. Later this same woman had admitted that she nearly didn't come to the meeting because she had eaten half a chocolate biscuit before she came, and she was sure she'd put on weight, and she'd cried and cried, but her friend persuaded her to go all the same.

Then, this. Apparently this woman, on one day, realized that she had mistakenly had four Amber Threes instead of three. So she had stuck her fingers down her throat to make herself sick. Anne thought this was hilarious. Stella was appalled. She would have taken this woman aside at the end of the meeting and explained to her that she needn't take it all quite so seriously. And she would have watched her carefully to see that she was not too neurotic to be dieting. But Anne relayed this anecdote around HQ purely for its amusement value. And this was the woman who wanted to be Area Co-ordinator.

Linda eased the pillow from beneath Stella's chest and instructed her to turn over. She did so, and now lay flat on her back, her breasts falling gently to each side. Another warm towel covered her body as Linda began to work on her face. Stella's jaw sagged and relaxed as Linda stroked her facial muscles. I must forget about Anne. How dare I let her spoil my afternoon off. Stella loved having her face massaged. It felt as if she were being shown infinite tenderness and affection, stroked and caressed by someone who loved her dearly. For one wild moment she let herself imagine it was Jo McKenzie who was massaging her, and murmuring that she was a gifted group leader, a lovely, warm person, someone very dear to her. Jo said that there was a special affinity between them, she wanted her to get the job. And most of all she wanted to meet her in a few weeks. Bubbles of excitement burst as Stella remembered Jo's impending visit. Perhaps she would meet her. Linda massaged her temples.

And then as Linda moved down to her collar bones the dream dissolved, to be replaced by a new nagging discomfort. There was something unpleasant that Stella had promised to do soon. What was it? Something she said she would do in October, and it was October now. And as Linda moved down the table to turn her attention to Stella's feet, she remembered. She had arranged to visit her parents in October. She was invaded by a familiar numb apathy. Linda pulled each toe individually. Her parents. Her father, never away from his table-tennis table in the front-room, or in fine weather, jogging around Valentine's Park. He loved her, in his inarticulate but undemanding way. And then there was her mother. All the tension that the massage had so successfully dispersed came flooding back. Linda covered all of Stella's body with the towel, and tactfully left the room so that she could dress.

As Stella fastened her bra at the back, an unwanted memory flashed into her mind. She was very small. The bathroom door was open and her mother was having a bath. She opened the door a little wider and peeked inside. Her mother had one leg balanced on the side of the bath, the flesh from her massive thigh hanging down, pitted and dimpled. She was bending over, washing her toes with attention. Large breasts hung down ramrod straight. Her stomach, her midriff, bulged and folded together as she bent over. Steam was everywhere. Stella saw with horror that her mother's bottom was hairy, dirty with hair. I don't want to be like that, thought the little girl. I don't want to be fat. She stood there transfixed. All that red mottled flesh, so ugly.

'Get out, Stella! Get out at once!'

Her mother had seen her. She vanished into her own bedroom. She had not realized how ugly a mummy's body could be. She would not let her body be like that. She would not be a mummy when she grew up. She would just live in a house with all of her dollies and look after them, and keep her body like it is now. With relief she pulled her track-suit top over her head. She was covered up and ready for Linda to return to bid her goodbye.

It was not Maureen's own idea to go to Woolworth's. The girls at the canteen had asked her to get a leaving card for Peggy, and she had agreed, of course. It was easier to go to Woolworth's because it was in the centre of Heyside, and the cards were right at the front of the shop, near the sweets. But Maureen was only going in to get a card. Since Peggy was only being transferred to another school kitchen – the one in Heyside Community College – Maureen thought she had better choose her a 'good luck' card. She would need it. It would be a far cry from St Mary's Primary.

She put the plastic-wrapped card in the wire basket she had collected from the front of the shop and stood indecisively in front of the pick 'n' mix. She told herself that she had lost five pounds last week and that she had been reasonably good this week. Why spoil it now with only one day to go? Maureen stood there hesitantly. It was hard for her to draw her attention away from the avalanche of Cadbury's Chocolate Eclairs. In Woolworth's you could get mint chocolate eclairs too. And plum chocolate creams. But nearly two weeks of Slim-Plicity and Stella's phone call last night had improved Maureen's resolve.

Of course. Jason and Kelly! Poor little lambs. Their naughty mummy (Maureen's daughter) never bought them any sweets. Nana would buy a little present for Jason and Kelly. Maureen moved over to the next unit where the sweet selection was aimed specifically at a younger market. A glass cabinet was divided into sections, and each contained a different kind of confectionery. There were foam strawberries, white chocolate mice, yellow chocolate bananas, My Little Pony chews for Kelly, tiny liquorice all-sorts, pink chocolate shrimps, jelly beans; Maureen's mouth watered. Using the plastic scoop provided, she filled two paper bags with sweets and took them to be weighed at the checkout, glowing with grandmotherly virtue. And, as she walked in the direction of Angie's flat, hoping that her daughter would be there, she refrained from sampling any of the contents of the paper bags, which she had put in the pocket of her coat.

When Maureen rang the doorbell of the flat, she heard footsteps and reflected with pleasure that she had caught them in. Angie was glad to see her. Maureen hung her coat up on the peg on the wall, and went into the lounge, where the two children were playing. Each stopped what they were doing, and each embraced one of Maureen's legs. They loved Nana. Maureen sunk down into Angie's low sofa, and the children clambered on top of her. She glanced at the clock on the wall opposite. Four o'clock. Quite wrong time to give the children sweets. It would spoil their tea and Angie would be none too pleased.

Maureen wondered idly what My Little Pony chews tasted like.

'Kelly, go and get Nana that picture you did at play group. It's in your bedroom.'

Kelly trotted off obediently, trailed by her younger brother. Maureen and Angie were disturbed by faint bangs and rumblings but, relieved to have the kids in a different room, they took no action; in their usual comfortable fashion, they exchanged the news of the day. Angie thought it was sad about Peggy, but at least it wasn't Maureen they'd tried to transfer. Maureen couldn't believe the price of children's shoes these days, but she agreed with Angie that you couldn't economize on something as important as shoes. The banging and rumbling had stopped. It was very quiet.

'Kelly? Jason? What are you up to? Come and watch television.'

The living-room door opened. Two small children walked in, their mouths smeared with different-coloured chocolate; in his tiny fist Jason clutched a pick 'n' mix bag. He looked innocently happy; his older sister's expression was uncertain.

'Where on earth did you get that from? Oh, mum, you didn't. I've told you before, we don't like the children having sweets. It spoils their teeth.'

'But they weren't for . . .' Maureen paused. 'Now. They were for later. I was going to give them to you to look after.'

'Oh, well, it can't be helped,' grinned Angie, as she switched on the television set.

Maureen prickled and thought she might have a hot flush coming on. She certainly felt very emotional.

Those naughty children. Fancy taking things from her pocket, even if she was going to give them the sweets later. They might have offered her some. She wondered what Angie thought of her. Maureen felt very hungry, but most of all she craved something sweet.

'Angie, I'd love a brew. You stay there, I'll make it.'

Maureen went into her daughter's kitchen, and plugged in the kettle. Swiftly she opened the pantry to see what Angie had in. Very little. She opened the biscuit tin. Empty. Damn. Maureen was angry, she felt she was owed something. The kettle began to hiss. She felt empty inside. She must eat something. She looked round the pantry again. It was a very large pantry, the sort you could step inside. She did. At her feet was a bag of potatoes and some bottles of Vimto. On the shelves opposite her were tins of beans, tins of soup, a tin of Campbell's meatballs. To her side were boxes of cereal; cornflakes, Weetabix, Coco Pops. Coco Pops. They would do. Maureen shut the pantry door and began to stuff handfuls of Coco Pops into her mouth. Really they needed sugar and they were a bit dry, but there certainly was a faint taste of chocolate. She took more. Her anger and disappointment were subsiding. In the far distance she heard the kettle click and turn itself off. She folded back the top of the Coco Pops and left the pantry. Calmly she proceeded to make a pot of tea. She had had her revenge.

CHAPTER SEVEN

Taking the knife in her right hand, Stella deftly scraped the excess low-fat spread from her one ounce of bread. The microwave gave its characteristic ping, and darkened. Stella took out her fish, and lifted the pink fillets on to the waiting plate. From the refrigerator Stella took a pack of ready-made salad that she had bought earlier that day at Marks & Spencer, and spooned precisely half on to her plate. She looked at it critically. There was perhaps a touch too much white cabbage, and she did not wish to feel bloated during the Slim-Plicity meeting that night. So she put some back into the plastic tray. Richard was at the Golf Club. Taking her plate, she went into the morning-room and prepared herself for a slow and enjoyable meal. Pink trout and salad, although expensive, was at least a meal that did not trigger off any uncomfortable guilt. Her first bite of the bread was very gratifying. She was really very hungry. She took another bite.

The phone rang.

Probably Richard, she thought, with mild irritation mixed with fondness. Or one of the Slim-Plicity clerks. She reluctantly pushed aside her meal, relieved that at least it would not spoil if it cooled.

'Hello, Stella, I just thought I'd give you a ring.'

It was her mother.

'Any news?'

A few months ago Stella had taken an assertiveness-training course, and learnt there that it was possible to tell unwanted callers on the telephone that you did not wish to speak to them just then, but would ring them back later. Once she had tried that on her mother. It hadn't worked. Her mother was not hurt or offended, or angry. She just continued talking. And now resentment prickled in Stella's fingers and toes.

'No news? Then tell me something interesting. Surely something has happened to you this week. How are your slimmers doing?'

It was an unanswerable question. Stella replied briefly. There was an awkward pause.

'And the office? Have they offered you any more classes?'

Stella's guilt at her unresponsiveness to her mother often led her to donate items of news that only led to further interrogation. She mentioned the vacancy for Area Co-ordinator.

'So tell me? Who's in the running?'

Stella told her.

'Anne? She's a friend of yours. Isn't she the very pretty one married to the chartered accountant? So will you get the job?'

Stella's reply was of course equivocal. Her stomach rumbled.

'When are the interviews?'

Stella said she didn't know and attempted to side-track her mother by asking a question herself.

'How's Dad?'

'All right. Do you want to speak to him?'

Stella didn't. Yet another uncomfortable pause.

'So when are you coming to visit us? You promised October. How about this weekend?'

Stella couldn't face it, and luckily it was one of Richard's weekends at home. But she knew that he was away on the twenty-seventh. Could she bear it, she wondered.

'What's wrong? Don't you want to come?'

Anything to avoid an argument. She would come on the twenty-seventh.

'Stella. I was reading the paper. Are you in the Slim-Plicity competition to meet what's-her-name? Joan McKenzie?'

Stella writhed with embarrassment and loathing. How dare she mention her name. She felt as she did when her mother quizzed her about her boyfriends. This was private. This was special. She felt her jaw clench, her toes curl.

'So you don't know yet? A shame. You look up to her, don't you?'

Stella tapped her foot. She would risk it.

'Mum, look, it's Thursday, the Heyside Slim-Plicity meeting. I've got to get ready. I'll ring you in the week to give you details about my visit. Okay?'

Her mother was mollified. Stella was able to put the phone down. Heavily she went back to her dinner. The fish had curled at the edges. She suppressed her feelings of dislike and instead allowed herself to be washed over by a wave of guilt. She should have more tolerance with her mother. She should answer her questions. Her mother needed to live vicariously through her. Her father offered little in the way of companionship. Stella resisted being pulled into thoughts about her parents' marriage. A dullness descended on her. Her food tasted ashen. Later, just before she packed the car for the Slim-Plicity meeting, she looked in the biscuit tin. There were the shortbread biscuits she had bought for Richard. She consumed one rapidly. It was crumbly and melting and forgave Stella for her impatience. She ate another. It relaxed her. She quickly had another. She jammed the lid back on the tin, and turned off the light in the kitchen.

Helen could feel her own impatience to get on the scales. Strange, because she hadn't thought it meant so much to her. But she was faintly irritated that there were at least eight women in front of her at the queue to get weighed. There was no sign of Sandra, who must have already been and gone, as it was well after seven. Helen took off her coat. She had made a special effort with her appearance tonight, she was going out with Sandra afterwards. She had put on a plain black skirt, which seemed to fit more comfortably, and a flowery blouse. She had washed her hair.

It was her turn at the scales. What if she hadn't lost anything? She was actually quite nervous. Then Stella looked up and beamed, as if she were giving her a present.

'That's another three pounds off.'

Helen was delighted. That was half a stone in a fortnight. She did not forget, however, to ask about Sandra. She had apparently lost a pound. Helen thought that she would not be too pleased about that. But Stella had looked quite happy when she had said it; clearly any weight loss was a good thing at Slim-Plicity.

Helen walked over to the semicircle of chairs surrounding the leader's table. She felt quite talkative, and so deliberately chose to sit next to a woman of about her own age who was alone at the end of a row; a tiny but stout lady with a short curly perm and wearing attractively framed glasses. She was dressed in a plain maroon skirt, a white filigree blouse, and had not yet taken off her navy three-quarter-length jacket. She smiled at Helen as she sat down next to her.

There was silence for a few moments. Helen decided on the conventional opening.

'Have you had a good week?'

'I've only joined tonight. Well, that is, rejoined. I was a member a couple of years ago, but I've put it back on since then.'

'Why was that?'

'No particular reason. I just can't resist sweet things. I can eat a whole packet of biscuits at a sitting. Greedy isn't the word!'

The woman smiled ruefully at Helen, and continued.

'I've just got no self-control, no will-power. I call myself Miss Piggy!'

She giggled. Helen smiled. The woman, glad to talk, went on.

'No, it's not funny really. I'm sick with myself. I look in the mirror and can't believe how I've let myself go. Look at all this fat!'

Helen was aware of a discrepancy now between this woman's image of herself and Helen's own perception of her. Helen saw a wry, humorous, attractive woman, whose obesity was not immediately obvious. The woman saw herself as a failure. And yet Helen had shared that self-loathing that seemed to be the result of excess flesh. And this self-loathing had diminished since she had lost her half stone. She noticed a wedding ring on the woman's hand.

'Do you have any children?'

'Yes. Two. Do you?'

'Yes. A son of five and a daughter of three. She'll be four soon.'

'My younger one is three. Toddlers are a handful, aren't they?'

'I find Katy the easier of the two. But that's because she's a girl. Matthew is a one-man destruction squad. How old is your other one?'

'He's nine.'

'Does it get any easier?' grinned Helen.

'Actually my son's a foster son. He's mentally handi-capped.'

Helen was stopped in her tracks. The woman continued.

'Simon has a mental age of eight months.' She smiled at Helen, acknowledging and dismissing her embarrass-ment.

I couldn't do that, Helen thought. She asked, 'What made you take him on?'

'It was before Jennifer came along. I saw an advert-isement in the local paper asking for foster parents and I applied.'

Stella moved up to the front of the room. For one disorientating moment Helen wondered what she was doing, trying to be like Stella, Judith and the svelte glamorous models of her magazines, when she admired

121

the woman sitting next to her so much more. And yet this woman was also trying to be slim and glamorous and . . . It just didn't make sense.

Stella began.

Stella had told her to see it in her mind's eye as two half-pounds of butter. But it made no difference. Sandra still felt acutely disappointed at only losing one pound. Yet there was this consolation. She was doubly determined to ally herself to the fortunes of the Fat Women's Support Group. She felt at one with them; they were her sisters; she could see the pitfalls of dieting; she too was a fat woman. She glanced around the Wellington, which was still quite empty. She recognized no one from the meeting a fortnight ago and hoped that she was not too early. That familiar feeling of being out of place, a fraction clumsy, overcame her. The elderly man collecting glasses noticed her hesitation and asked if he could help her. Reddening, she asked if she was too early for the Fat Women's Support Group.

The man looked at her quizzically.

'You're too slim to be one o' them,' he stated with a Mancunian directness.

Sandra immediately felt better. With rising spirits, she found out that already some of the women had arrived, and she made her way upstairs to the room at the end of the corridor. She entered, and found Liz Breen, Martha, Emma and one other. She smiled at them, still unsure.

Liz greeted her heartily.

'It's Sandra, isn't it? It's good you've come. Take a chair. We're expecting a few others.'

Sandra did as she was told and was encouraged by the comforting smile of the pretty blonde woman – Emma, was it? – who seemed this week to be radiating well-being. Yet again Sandra realized that it was possible to be fat and beautiful. Liz broke into her reverie.

'Well, Sandra, since you're early, you can tell us a bit about yourself. Just as much as you feel comfortable with. What are your personal reasons for coming to join us?'

With the swiftness of a word processor deleting unwanted phrases, Sandra edited her life. There was to be no mention of Slim-Plicity, of her other attempts to diet, of Helen (for now), of her boyfriend Dave . . . she began.

'I'm twenty. I'm living in Middleton and I'm a student at the university. I've been overweight since a teenager and my self-consciousness about it has been a real problem to me. I enjoy eating . . . I belong to a women's group,' she spoke more quickly, 'and then I began to realize that the fault did not lie in myself, but in a society that insists that a woman's prime function is the preparation and provision of food, yet forbids her from indulging herself in it.'

Liz nodded. Sandra gained confidence.

'It seems to me that a fat woman is made to feel a misfit. I feel a misfit. At the bad times I feel different and worse than all my friends because I'm fat. I want to learn to accept myself.'

Sandra could feel herself getting quite emotional. This was partly because she still felt awkward talking openly to these new acquaintances, and partly because she realized that she had accidentally hit upon a truth.

She did feel different and worse than her friends. And she wondered how deeply this inadequacy went. She might allow herself the luxury of talking about it to Cathy . . . or Helen. Liz put her arm around Sandra in a chummy way.

'We're glad you've joined us. And you won't be a misfit here.'

Sandra was subliminally insulted, but reprimanded herself stiffly for that momentary aberration. She watched the door open and three more women walk in. They took their places around the large conference table.

Martha said 'Shall we begin?'

Liz began.

Stella looked round at her audience and established eye contact with every part of it.

'I feel good,' she said, 'because I'm slim and in control. Not in control of you,' she laughed, 'but in control of myself. I'm in control of my eating.' She decided to forget about the biscuits earlier.

'Being in control is about discipline – learning to live by certain rules and limits. That's what we've all got to do if we're going to succeed at this slimming business. In every part of life there are rules and we've got to obey them. You drive on the left of the road; you don't go to work in your pyjamas; you fill in the cheques in your cheque book in the way you're instructed to. And it's the same with losing weight. You won't lose weight unless you stick to the rules. And the rules are in your manual. Now in my experience the rule that is most often broken is the one regarding weighing. Of course, we all come here to get weighed, and that's a vital part of your slimming. Without the incentive that the scales provide, you wouldn't stick to it. But just as important as regularly weighing yourself is weighing your food. Do you check how much that slice of bread that you all eat first thing in the morning actually weighs? Is it one ounce? Not if it comes from a thick-sliced loaf. Do you put that slice of bread on the scales? You should. And that apple you have after lunch. How much does that weigh? A Slim-Plicity apple must only weigh four ounces – no more, no less. Most apples you buy in supermarkets are more than that. Have a knife at the ready by your scales to pare off that extra amount. Weigh your Amber Threes. Fat makes you fat.

'So many times I have Slim-Plicity members get on the scales and tell me that they've had a good week, and then they don't lose as much as they hoped, or might even gain. And the reason is that they have not been careful about quantities. Weigh your food as well as yourselves. It's just a matter of discipline. But the one thing that is immeasurable is the feeling of pride and well-being you get when you realize that you have been good, and that you are in control.'

Liz began. For Sandra's benefit she once more stated the aims of the group.

'I feel good because I'm fat and in control. There is nothing wrong with being fat. In fact fat women are generally women who love life, love food – cooking, sharing, giving food – and have a genuine sensual appreciation of what they eat. To be fat is to choose not to compete in this competitive society. And when you have chosen to be fat you are free from the tyranny of the judgement of others. I am in control of my own eating, not the scales, not the critical eyes of society (although the battle against anti-fat remarks is one we wage constantly). Real control is the exercise of personal freedom. I do not want any authority to tell me how I ought to eat.'

Martha, an anarchist, nodded vehemently. Liz continued.

'I eat according to the needs of my body, my moods. Who dares tell me that at the end of a hard day working in the women's refuge I don't deserve – and need – a good, satisfying meal. In this group we all choose to look the way we want, and eat the way we want, and we take control and responsibility for our own bodies, and we construct an environment in which we can support each other's decisions. We enjoy being fat and are proud to be fat.'

Stella saw an arm waving tentatively at the back of the rows of women. She gave her permission to speak.

'My problem, Stella, is that I think I'm getting obsessed with this diet.'

Some women around her nodded.

'I seem to be thinking about it all day long. I'm always working out how much food I've got left in each category, and always thinking about how much weight I might have lost by the end of the week. My husband says I'm getting really boring.'

'But I bet he prefers you the way you look now! Seriously, Eunice, you mustn't let yourself get obsessed. You'll only make yourself miserable. Find something else to think about. Take up crocheting or something. Remember, all of you, that dieting is only part of your life. It's the most important part, but it's only part.'

'Now, Emma,' smiled Liz, 'I know you have a particular issue that you wish to raise tonight, and everyone has agreed that it should form the main part of our agenda. So over to you.'

Emma looked fractionally nervous. She glanced quickly at Martha. Martha sat with her arms folded and her lips pursed. Sandra immediately sensed the antagonism between them and was curious. She felt an instinctive liking for Emma, and so listened to her argument with sympathy.

'First I want to say that I agree with everything Liz has just said. I enjoy eating, and I enjoy making my own decisions about food and weight. But as nearly all of you know, I've put on a lot of weight fairly recently, because of the difficulties I've been having in my relationship with my husband. Well, I'm leaving him.'

'Good!' said Liz and Martha in unison.

'Since making that decision, and due to several other reasons, I've been eating less, and I've lost a bit of weight without intending to. That makes me feel happy. And if I'm being absolutely honest, I don't enjoy overeating. When I binge on food because I'm miserable I don't like doing it. I don't taste what I eat and I don't like myself afterwards. Nobody could be more against the idea of dieting than me, but I would like the group's help in not eating when I'm in the grip of a binge. I've been reading *Fat is a Feminist Issue* again. I like the book very much. It's about not eating when you're not hungry, and explores why so many women suffer from a food/weight obsession. What I'm trying to say is that I'd like the rest of the group to read the book too, and perhaps to work along the lines Susie Orbach suggests, exploring our own relationship with food and the underlying reasons for obesity. Perhaps we could . . .'

'Count me out,' interrupted Martha. 'I've read *Fat is a Feminist Issue*. It's just another diet book. The women who buy it do so because they want to lose weight. The point about our Fat Women's Support Group is that we're happy with the way we are NOW, and we challenge the accepted stereotypes of society. Susie Orbach doesn't. She doesn't question the fact that it's desirable to be slim. We do. We're proud to be fat, and in that pride we show our solidarity with all oppressed groups. Gay women and black women don't read books where the end result is to stop being black or gay. Fat is political.'

'Fat is personal,' countered Emma.

'The personal is political,' said Liz, evenly, trying to restore harmony. Sandra felt brave enough to make a contribution.

'Can't we do both? I mean, do some of the things in *Fat is a Feminist Issue* and be proud we're fat?'

Martha ignored her.

'We've got to *show* that we're proud to be fat. It's time we took some direct action. We must strike a blow at the heart of society.'

Liz looked up with interest. Emma looked at Sandra and smiled wearily. Martha continued.

'We've spent too long sitting talking in this room. We've got to get out on the streets. We've got to make our presence felt.'

'But there aren't enough of us for a demo,' said Liz.

'No, but there's enough of us for a picket. We'll demonstrate outside a clothes shop – one of those shops that caters for no one over size sixteen. Where shall we go?'

A voice suggested 'C & A's?'

'I don't think so,' interjected Liz. 'I saw a jacket there in a size twenty-six once.'

'What about Du Mont?' said another.

'Yes!' cried Sandra excitedly. 'Even the fourteens are scarce there, and they stock a wide range of size eights!'

'Excellent!' said Martha. 'They cater exclusively for slim women, and perpetrate the outrages done against fat women. They maintain the myth that only slim women can be beautiful.'

'That's very provocative, Martha. We'll cause trouble for ourselves rather than do good,' Emma said softly.

But it was no use. Liz's imagination was fired too.

'I know what you mean, Emma, but just think of the inspiration we'll be to all the thousands of fat women shopping that day who have been afraid to come out and announce that they want to give up dieting and be proud to be fat. This is a wonderful idea. I vote we give it a try. What do you think, Sandra?'

'It's ever so interesting.'

'Let's have a vote. All those in favour . . .' Liz saw that only Emma's hand did not go up.

'Carried! We'll picket Du Mont. I know you've got reservations, Emma, but please join us. You've chosen to be part of us – be positive!'

'You've chosen to be part of us – be positive!' Stella looked at every member of her audience as she said her concluding words. She caught Helen's eye and smiled at her. She knew Helen to be one of her best losers, and this triggered off one last thought.

'We've had a good week this week, which means that we're well on target for November twenty-ninth.'

The group looked at her, baffled.

'What's special about the twenty-ninth?' Stella asked them, sensing she had lost them.

Silence.

'That's six weeks hence . . .'

'Is it your birthday, Stella?' ventured one brave lady.

'No, dear. But it's the closing date of the Slim-Plicity autumn competition. All the weight we lose in the next six weeks could help us win a celebration buffet in a big hotel. So far our average weight loss per person is 1.85 pounds. We can improve that and show that we're the best slimming group in the north-west. Next week, when you're dithering over whether to have that forbidden biscuit, think of your fellow members and diet for all of us. Good night, ladies.'

'So it's Du Mont in the Arndale Centre. When shall we do it?' asked Liz.

'It will have to be a Saturday for it to have maximum impact.' Sandra was beginning to get carried away.

'Damn!' said Martha. 'I'm working for the next few Saturdays.' Martha was part of the collective that ran Beano, a local wholefood shop.

'When are you free again?' inquired Liz.

Martha consulted her *Spare Rib* diary. 'November the tenth.'

'That will do fine. Anyway, it's getting near Christmas and the shops will be busy. An excellent time. Also we'll avoid the Guy Fawkes dummies . . .'

'I think we're the dummies,' muttered Emma, to no one in particular.

Liz continued. 'I'll see to the organization, and I'll contact you during the week, Martha, if I run into any difficulties. There are the leaflets, of course. We'll have to have some leaflets printed for handing out. Any volunteers?'

Liz was flushed with excitement and her normally wide smile widened. She was never happier than when she was involved in plotting and planning. Sandra had caught her excitement, but now glanced guiltily at Emma who was sitting quietly, but composed, at the end of the table. As the meeting broke up, Emma smiled at her.

'Are you doing anything now, Sandra?'

'I'm meeting a friend here for a drink, if it's nine o'clock.'

'That's a shame. I was going to ask you if you'd have a drink with me. My mini-cab isn't picking me up until ten, so I have an hour to kill.'

'Have a drink with us! Please do; Helen won't mind at all, in fact she'd be delighted.'

Sandra was thoroughly enjoying herself. The

meeting was exciting and productive. She had made a new, glamorous friend, *and* she was going to have a drink with her and Helen. She felt momentarily that it was no bad thing that she had a weight problem. Almost as if because she had a weight problem – and of course it wasn't a problem – she had met all these interesting people. As she and Emma descended the stairs she noticed Helen standing hesitantly at the main door of the Wellington. Of course! She should have realized that Helen was just the sort of woman who would not like going into pubs alone. Sandra quickly approached her.

Helen's mind was a blur of confused impressions. Just now, sitting alone, while Sandra had returned to the bar for another round, and Emma had gone to the Ladies, she was alone with time to think. She had never realized that there were women who actually wanted to be fat. And she did have to admit that Emma was quite beautiful. But picketing Du Mont! It seemed childish to her and she wished that Sandra wasn't involved. She also realized with a sense of wonder that she had spent time with two other women without talking about the children (her permanent focus of interest) or household affairs. That was quite exhilarating. And the pleasure she was having seemed quite separate from the earlier pleasure of the weight loss. Sitting here in the Wellington, she felt quite daring; Helen Greenwood as an individual, separate and distinct from her children and husband, talking with two other women about picketing a shop in Manchester! Sandra returned with the drinks.

Helen sipped at hers, and her attention wandered as

Emma and Sandra spoke of a mutual acquaintance. The three women were sitting in a booth towards the back of the pub, and Helen could see the bar facing her and most of the right-hand side of the drinking area. Idly she watched people drinking, talking, gesturing. Then she saw, making his way among the crowd, someone *she* knew. It was her next-door neighbour. She smiled at him. But despite the fact he was coming towards her he did not seem to see her. He approached Emma and stood by her, putting his hand protectively on her shoulder. Emma turned, and looked up at him, her face suddenly alight with pleasure. For that moment only they two were in the room. And then Len noticed Helen.

There was one moment of infinite silence. Emma broke it.

'I'm afraid my cab's here now. I'll have to go. I'll see you next week, Sandra. It was lovely meeting you, Helen.'

Helen and Len exchanged a strained smile as Emma got up, took Len's hand, and left with him.

'Do you like her?' asked Sandra with enthusiasm.

'Well, Len Pearce certainly does. He's my next-door neighbour. And he's married.'

'Wow!'

Helen was speechless. Clearly there was something between them. Did Judith know? She'd seen very little of Judith recently. But the irony! Judith had lost all that weight, and here was Len seeing a woman who was fatter than his wife before she had lost her excess weight. Well, she thought to herself, whether you decide to diet or not to diet, it's certainly not worth doing it for a man.

'Helen, apart from that, what did you think of Emma? I suppose I mean, what did you think of what she said, her ideas – our ideas,' Sandra corrected herself. 'Are you going to carry on with Slim-Plicity?'

'Yes. Since I've chosen to do it I might as well carry on with it. I feel like being positive for a bit.'

The edifice of certainty about the cause of fat women that Sandra had been building crumbled instantly. Her face fell. Helen noticed this.

'But you don't have to, Sandra. It's a matter of personal choice. You can choose to do whatever you want.'

'I think I might come with you to Slim-Plicity next week, Helen.'

'And the picket?'

'Oh, I think I'll do that too.'

CHAPTER EIGHT

Stella parked her car at the back of the shops, and, taking her suitcase from the boot, went towards the opening that led to the Parade itself. The Parade was quiet. That was to be expected; it was half past three on a Saturday afternoon, and anyway, most shoppers nowadays went to the larger supermarkets, or to nearby Romford. She walked past the newsagent, a hardware store, a video shop (surely that was new?), the chemist and finally arrived at Marie's Fashions. The exterior of the shop was unpromising. It was double-fronted and hopelessly old-fashioned. Tired, bored-looking mannequins stood adorned with drab suits in maroon and grey; one was clutching the hand of a stiff, marbled child dressed in plain shorts and a T-shirt. In the second window two more child models were clothed untidily in the local school uniforms; one bottle green, one navy blue. A few ladies' blouses were hung at the back of each window display. And yet Stella paused to look at the mannequins with something like affection. Their distant ennui was familiar to her; she had grown up with them. She walked into the shop.

To her surprise the shop was full. Her mother was serving an elderly lady, presumably with lingerie – Stella's mother's personal euphemism for corsets. In addition there was a mother with two small boys, with her father in attendance, and another relatively young woman waiting to be served. Stella smiled at her parents, indicated that she did not need immediate attention, and looked around her.

The shop counters formed a square U-shape around the sides of the shop. They were glass-fronted, and behind the sliding doors were trays of underwear: socks, knickers, slips. Behind the counters was open shelving half full of ladies' blouses, children's T-shirts, with sticky labels coded to show the price. To Stella's left were several rails of larger items of clothing; ladies' suits, items of school uniform, old-fashioned ruched swim-suits. There was a sweet, musty smell. Stella was overcome with familiarity and revulsion. She watched the mother of the two children shake her head, take hold of her two small children, and drag them out of the shop. As her father turned to the waiting customer, Stella indicated that she would wait in the back. She lifted the flap that formed a continuation of the counter at the back of the shop, and went into the tiny back-room, cluttered with boxes. She sat on the hard wooden chair that was positioned to look out into the shop through a small hatch. She would have liked a coffee, but down here, although there was a sink and a kettle, she could only see a box of tea-bags, sugar, a bottle of maturing milk, and two mugs, both ringed from previous cups of tea. She closed in on herself and watched her parents like a spy.

Her father was so slow; his dithering as he attempted to serve his customer was characteristic. Stella could detect her impatience. She watched her father throw the occasional anxious glance over to her mother. She knew why. Should he make a mistake, she was implacable. Every little slip he made, whether it was in pricing, replacing stock in the correct way, or returning burnt matchsticks to the matchbox when he had used them for lighting his pipe, every mistake was remarked upon, docketed, and stored away for some final judgement day. And in his simplicity and admiration for the superior abilities of his wife, Harry Conway had never questioned this. He tried hard never to incur her wrath, and kept out of her way as much as possible. Stella felt sorry for him, and frustrated by him.

Her mother had shifted so that she was momentarily standing directly in Stella's line of vision, and she could only see her back. Marie Conway was wearing a grey dress with a pattern of small sprigs of flowers in peach and pink; the skirt was pleated. The viscose material clung to her mother's ample outline, and Stella could see where the top of her mother's corset began – her flesh bulged slightly at the top. Her mother moved away to the corner of the shop and was out of view. Stella felt resigned. What Richard had said was true; she was lucky. She had managed to escape from her mother by going to live in the north, and one weekend was a small price to pay. Surely one could put up with incessant questioning for twenty-four hours. She noticed how Richard often chose not to come with her on these visits, and it wasn't so bad for him. It wasn't just the questioning; there was more to it than that.

Stella felt her mother wanted to possess her. Her interrogations were a way of storing information, gaining control. At the end of most visits Stella felt as if she had been broken up and reassembled in the pattern that her mother wanted. She was always conscious of the tremendous pressure to please, to feed her mother with what she craved. And what was it she craved? Why was it that Stella was so conscious of the pressure of resisting her mother's demands? At times it was as if her mother wanted to consume her entirely. Stella knew that if she did not erect a barrier she would be swallowed up whole.

It wasn't that her mother wanted her to be, or to do, anything in particular. She wasn't expected to become a doctor or a lawyer, or save the world. That was perhaps because she was not a boy. But her mother wanted to share with her every last detail of her life. She remembered vividly one night when she must have been thirteen, or fourteen? Her parents had been to school for the annual parents' evening. Stella attended the local girls' grammar school; a bit of an anachronism in those days of the pioneer comprehensive schools. But Stella liked it. She was of average ability, loved drama and being in school plays, and thoroughly enjoyed the network of friendships, the individual teachers, their foibles and personalities. It was so much more interesting than home.

Her parents came back that night – she remembered her father just sitting there grinning – and her mother smiling with contentment. But it wasn't because Stella had done well. It was because her mother had gained access to her school life . . .

'Your English teacher is very pretty – I didn't think the way she was dressed was very suitable, though. Fancy wearing a full-length skirt to a parents' evening. But she's friendly, I will say that. We got on very well. I suppose if I'd had a teacher like that I might not have left school at fourteen. We didn't have the opportunities you youngsters have got today. Oh, I wanted to take my matric, believe me, but your grandmother wouldn't hear of it. Isn't your biology teacher old? Would you believe it, she drives a sports car. I saw her get into it at the end.'

'Mum, what did they say about me?'

'You're doing perfectly all right. Could try harder, though. Reminds me of myself at your age. I liked French. I could have been quite fluent given the opportunity. Was that your painting in the art room? I suppose you call that modern art. Your art teacher seemed to think it was okay, but I don't know, I don't understand these things. Give me a nice old-fashioned picture any time . . .'

That night, when her parents had settled themselves in front of the television, Stella had gone into the kitchen and eaten biscuit after biscuit. She was consumed with self-hatred . . .

It must have been around the same time she started going out with Roger, her first boyfriend. How thrilling that was, despite his acne, and the ultraviolet lamp treatment he had to have for it, which left his face permanently red! Stella smiled. And that was when her mother's interrogations really got under way . . .

'So, where did you go? To the pictures – the pictures, she says! What pictures? The Odeon? The ABC? What was on? I wouldn't fancy that myself. Did you like it?' More suspiciously . . . 'Where did you sit? And did he try anything?'

'Oh, Mum!'

'Because I wouldn't let him get fresh yet. I'd been

going out with Stan for quite a few weeks before I let him kiss me. And I was older than you. So, have you met his mother? What's she like? What did she give you to eat? Are they well off? What does his father do? Doesn't he work in the City?'

She heard the shop bell ring. That meant another customer had left. In a moment Stella's mother was in the back-room embracing her daughter. Stella had to bend her head forward slightly to compensate for the fact that her mother's bust was so large that it was impossible to hug her closely. Her mother's cheek was soft and slack.

'Why didn't you wait upstairs, Stella? You could have eaten. I've been shopping.'

Ominous words. This was what Stella had been dreading. Yes – there were the interrogations, but also her mother's other weapon – food. Food was the means by which Marie Conway exerted her authority, wielded power in the home. Naughty girls weren't allowed to eat; good girls were. Happy times meant big meals; when Harry and Marie weren't on speaking terms it was just beans on toast. And when you had eaten anything that Marie had cooked you were in her power . . .

'You haven't said thank you for that lovely fish . . .'

'Now I've made you your dinner come and talk to me . . .'

'I've bought a cheesecake just for you, Stella. Come upstairs with me now and we can make a start on it. I've got so much I want to ask you.'

Stella followed her mother up the wooden stairs, with the turn in them, to the flat above the shop. She watched her mother's hips swaying, and heard her mother's painful breathing. When Marie reached the top of the stairs she paused to catch her breath.

'Well, I don't get any younger.'

Both women went into the small kitchen. The room only had one high window looking out over an alleyway that connected a delivery area with the Parade. Marie put the kettle on. There was nowhere for Stella to sit so she stood, feeling large and ill at ease, in her mother's kitchen. She knew she was not allowed to help. Marie chattered on.

'Would you believe it? The one Saturday you come home, we're busy in the shop. Every other weekend we've been so slack you wouldn't credit it. I don't know where they're all going to? And the rubbish you buy in these chain stores. How's Richard? Is he still doing all that travelling? I don't know how you put up with it? Did you get the job at your slimming club? It's a blackcurrant cheesecake; I bought it, didn't have time to make it; with your father out every evening I'm busy ticketing the stock by myself. He's coaching a boy, would you believe, at the sports club. Table-tennis, of course. Do you take sugar? Of course not – your diet. So how is your diet? If you don't mind me saying so, you look far too thin. You need a good hot meal to build you up. I don't hold with all this dieting. In the war . . .'

Once more Stella retreated into herself. One didn't actually have to listen to Marie; sometimes it was enough just to be there. Her talking was compulsive – like her eating, thought Stella, as she watched her mother make herself a thick cheese sandwich and eat it as she prepared the tea.

'I haven't had a chance to eat all day,' she said, in explanation.

Marie continued to talk as she ate. Stella tried hard to control her disgust. She glanced at the kitchen clock. It was still only just past four. She would have to wait some time before she could see her father. A lot of her childhood had been spent waiting for her father. It was either long hours in the shop, or evenings playing table-tennis, visiting friends ... she often wondered how it was she had ended up marrying a man who she was also permanently waiting for, as Richard departed on yet another business trip.

'So where has Richard gone this time?'

'Germany.'

'I wouldn't fancy that myself,' said Marie, as she swallowed the last of her sandwich. 'Come into the front-room and eat.'

Stella followed her mother into the front-room, a lounge-cum-dining-room that extended the whole length of the shop. It was a sunny room, though the furniture was dated, and the fabrics faded. But for Stella it was all inexplicably comforting. However ambivalent she was about her childhood it certainly felt safe and familiar to be back on the Parade. She sat down at the table with her mother, who cut into the cheesecake. Stella took a silver fork and began to eat, accompanied by her mother. Faintly in the distance they heard the shop bell ring once, then twice. Marie put her fork down.

'I'd better go and see what your father's up to. I can't trust him down there.'

Alone Stella returned to the cheesecake with renewed enthusiasm. She ate it slowly and with great pleasure. Each mouthful was exquisite, as it melted and soothed. The sweetness was exciting, balanced against the tartness of the acidic fruit. With her finger, Stella pressed down on her plate and picked up the crumbs, and ate those too. She took the cake knife and cut herself just another small sliver. It was not quite as nice as the first time, but still it was good. She had just a little more.

A few moments later Stella realized that her usual empty feeling had gone. She was no longer hungry. She panicked. What had she done? She went to her mother's bathroom and pulled out the old black scales from under the sink. The black plastic adhered to the soles of her stockinged feet. Nine stone seven: Oh, God! That can't be right. I was only nine one this morning, she thought. Stella's mind raced. Was it the cheesecake? Or were these scales wrong? Probably. They were rarely used. But what if *her* scales were wrong? What if she really was nine seven? It was unthinkable. Come on, she told herself, no one puts on six pounds in half a day. She heard footsteps and hastily left the bathroom, pulling the chain as she did so.

It was her father. He hugged her closely.

'How are you, Dad?'

'Not so bad. Up and down.'

He grinned at her. Stella smiled back.

'It's good to see you, Dad.'

There was a pause.

'So how have you been keeping, Stella?'

'Fine. And you?'

'Not so bad.'

'How's the table-tennis?'

'Coming along.'

He grinned and scratched the back of his neck, a characteristic gesture. He glanced at the sideboard where his pipe, and his Dutch tobacco, lay undisturbed.

'It's nice to get away from her,' he said.

Don't tell me this, thought Stella. I don't want to know. As an only child she had frequently been ground to pieces by the constant friction between her parents. Each, trusting her, had used her as a confidante, and when she was quite young, Stella had lost her trust in each.

'It's a hard life,' he said, fishing again. 'She keeps me at it.'

All right. So it was true. Marie ruled Harry like a tyrant. And when she was alone with Richard she would talk about this and sympathize with her father. But with him, sympathy was an act of betrayal. And moreover, had he not brought it on himself? Few could be patient with his shambling incompetence, least of all Marie.

'And how *is* the table-tennis, Dad?'

'I've found a promising youngster to coach. Craig. A nice boy. Do you think I've got time for a smoke?'

'I don't know.'

'She might want me downstairs . . . if she's busy. Shall I . . . ?'

Stella remained silent.

'Your mother has a temper on her . . .'

The shop bell rang.

'I'd better . . .'

And then Harry went into the bathroom and locked the door. Stella was both amused and irritated. She waited. There was no sound. Harry was going to be in there for a long time. This was just what Stella had been expecting. Unwilling to go back to the shop, but equally unwilling to face the consequences, he would spend twenty minutes in the bathroom as a meek protest. Or perhaps there really was something wrong with his bowels. She would never know. Certainly he had been suffering from this complaint since her childhood . . .

'Harry! Where on earth have you put the girls' socks? Have you unpacked them yet? Harry? Where are you?'

'He's in the bathroom, Mum.'

Or . . .

'Somebody's priced the vests wrongly . . . they're one ninety-nine, not ninety-nine. Harry? Harry!'

'Sorry, Mum, he said he'd got a stomach ache.'

Stella pulled herself back to the present moment, in time to hear her mother's voice from below.

'Stella! Tell your father to come down immediately. I need his help.'

'Sorry, Mum, he's in the bathroom. But I'll come.'

Stella hurried downstairs, glad to be able to do something. She enjoyed serving in the shop. As a child she felt privileged to serve. And now that she had learned to derive so much pleasure from her public face, as a group leader, her happiest times were those when she interacted with strangers. In addition, working side by side with her mother in the shop was a way to restore harmony. She lifted the counter top,

and approached the two waiting West Indian women.
'Can I help you?'

Stella stood on the shop floor in the semi-darkness as
her mother opened the side door. It was Sunday morning. As usual, Marie was going to the baker's for some
bagels. Sunday was her day of rest, her eating day.
Stella had agreed to accompany her on the short walk
to Lipman's. The fresh shock of the cold autumn air
was pleasant. The wind ruffled Stella's hair and cooled
her. Her mother commenced her monologue.

'So then your Auntie Milly told me that it was my
fault for interfering. Have you ever heard such a thing!
So I told her that somebody had to say something, and
she should be old enough to look after herself . . .'

As she walked along the street, Stella's mother
occasionally bumped into her. She seemed to walk
diagonally, and to be careless of the space between her
and her daughter, as if it were of no account. Stella
found herself walking nearer and nearer to the shop
fronts. But she walked in a stupor. She was not listening to her mother; she was trapped in her old nightmare. Three pieces of cheesecake, a large portion of
lasagne, ice-cream, four chocolate biscuits. Four chocolate biscuits, ice-cream, a large portion of lasagne, three
pieces of cheesecake. It was unbearable to contemplate.
This morning on her parents' scales she had weighed
nine eight. Whether the scales were wrong or right,
she had put on a pound. She was a pig, a disgusting
pig. They entered the baker's.

There was a small queue inside the shop which
moved quickly, as there were plenty of girls behind

the counter. On Stella's left was a display of various cakes and biscuits; in front of her was the main counter, behind which were stacks of different sorts of breads: white loaves, rye bread, granaries, bloomers, and of course to one side were the bagels. Stella loved bagels. So did Marie. To Stella their sweet firmness reminded her of many a happy Sunday lunch-time before she learnt about dieting; for Marie too they re-created a childhood of tradition and security. Marie bought a dozen and then the two women went next door to the delicatessen for smoked salmon, chopped herring, cream cheese. Stella was mesmerized.

Saturday night had been quiet. Harry had watched television, and Stella had suggested to her mother that they play Scrabble. Marie played with a fierce competitiveness which prevented her from talking to any great extent. They all had an early night. And yet Stella had eaten the lasagne, the cheesecake, ice-cream and, unforgivably, four chocolate biscuits.

Back at the flat they prepared lunch. It was good to cut and spread the bagels with butter, good to top them with thick layers of chopped herring and cream cheese. Small segments of cucumber sat astride the cream cheese like little green rafts on a white ocean. As they worked the women became companionable . . .

'So I told them at the warehouse they could stick their fancy blouses you-know-where. The cheek of it, charging that much!'

'Don't go there again, Mum.'

'You can bet your life I won't. Did I tell you that they said Milly's got high blood pressure? It was when she went to get her eyes tested. Ten pounds they charge these days, it's criminal. So as I was saying, they gave her all the tests, and her cataracts were small, but would you believe it, she's got high blood pressure. And if you ask me, it's looking after your cousin's children that does it. Where's your father?'

'I don't know.'

'Why am I asking you? It's Sunday morning – he'll be out jogging. A stranger he is. And at his age why bother to look after your figure?'

Carefully Stella stacked the bagels on a large plate. She remembered when Milly and Rosemary would come for tea, and she and Rosemary would take a plate of bagels between them, and sit with them behind the settee to talk. Once they stole a knife and cut all the bagels into tiny pieces (for their dolls) and all but ruined the carpet. Marie had been furious. Stella was about to share this memory with her mother when the door to the flat opened and, panting, Harry ran in.

Twenty minutes later all were seated round the table. Certainly Stella's mood had improved. For one, she was leaving in a couple of hours. She had also planned to have only two halves of the bagels to compensate for her over-indulgence yesterday. But, most of all, there had been no arguments. Perhaps all of them were mellowing.

'Don't you think the chopped herring is a bit salty, Stella?'

'Tastes fine to me.'

'Harry. You find it salty?'

Harry was eating, and shook his head.

'So, Stella, you've hardly spoken about Richard. What's he doing? How is he?'

'Okay. Working hard.'

'Do you know what he does in the office?'

'Writing reports, speaking on the telephone – what do you mean?'

'Well, you see these programmes on television. You never know what these businessmen get up to. You know he's not a Jewish boy.'

'Mum! Don't be ridiculous.' (That's just too absurd to upset me, thought Stella.)

'Mind you, Rosemary married a Jewish boy and look what happened. And now tell me about your work. So you didn't get that job?'

'You mean Area Co-ordinator? The interviews aren't for a while.'

'And will it be full time?'

Stella had eaten her two halves of bagels, but she was still hungry. Perhaps one more . . .

'Because I don't think it's such a good idea if it's full time. You don't want to work as hard as I've had to.'

This time Stella took a smoked salmon bagel. Perhaps there were fewer calories.

'And you've been married four years. Your father and I would love some grandchildren.'

This time Stella chose a cream cheese bagel.

'You're not having problems, are you? All your old school friends are having babies.'

Just one more chopped herring.

'Tell me about your friend Anne. How is she these days? Still as pretty as ever?'

This smoked salmon bagel really would be the last.

'Steady on there, Stella. You're not leaving any bagels for anyone else!'

The bagel turned to ashes in Stella's mouth. It was true. She had overeaten. How dare her mother point it out – the hypocrite. Look at her, eating too, and well over fourteen stone. She felt like striking her mother. She hated her with an overpowering hatred. But most of all she hated herself. She could have stuck knives in herself. Her skin prickled. Her anger surged like a wave, and fell back, and dissolved into tears that welled up and would not be repressed.

'You've had just as many, Mum.'

'So what are you crying about? It's not so terrible.'

'It is to me and you know it. Throw them all away!'

Stella stormed out of the room and flung herself on the bed in the spare bedroom, just as she did when she was a girl. And she despised herself for this welter of emotion. It was what her mother wanted. When Marie had resurrected the child in Stella, she was satisfied. She was badly hurt by her mother's insensitivity and lack of understanding. Eating too much! And yet, the worst thing of all was that it was true. She had eaten six half-bagels. She would be fat again. Flesh would surround her and wobble as she walked. She did not trust her own body. And she sobbed and sobbed.

Once she had left the M25 and was heading north on the M1 Stella felt her inner tension dissolving. As the distance grew that separated her from her parents, her sense of perspective returned. How could I, she thought. How despicable to give in to her mother's constant needling with that ugly outburst. If only she hadn't mentioned food. Stella resolved firmly not to eat for the rest of the day, and took a grim pleasure in doing so. By not eating she felt she was defying her mother.

But then, she thought, is eating pleasing my mother? That analysis didn't feel right. Often eating for her was an anodyne, an escape, a way of shutting things out. It was a way of erecting a barrier and shutting her mother out. It used to feel like that. But then, of course, when she realized what damage she'd done to her body, she redirected all her anger at herself. And then she would eat more. Or at least it was like that until she joined Slim-Plicity. Then she saw that the rigour of dieting was a sufficient punishment for being fat, and the control and discipline necessary put up another sort of barrier between her and her mother. Her mother would never diet. Stella knew that slimness was a reproach to her mother, a gesture of defiance.

Driving along the motorway always restored her composure. She enjoyed feeling in control of her Escort Cabriolet, and took pride in her careful, professional driving. In her car, she always felt she was Stella Martin, Slim-Plicity group leader, successful and admired by thousands of women all over the north-west. She had no connection with her mother. Cars flashed by in the fast lane, separately. Whatever the scales said tonight when she reached home would not upset her. She straightened her shoulders imperceptibly.

Perhaps she and Heyside would win the autumn promotion. There was no reason why not. She would walk up to Jo McKenzie, watched by all the Heyside members, and shake her hand. Jo would smile at her and as their eyes met, there would be a moment of recognition. And later, as the buffet went on, they would talk. Jo would congratulate her on her record at Slim-Plicity.

'You were my inspiration, Jo. I wanted to do in England, in Manchester, what you have done in the States.'

Jo would have a soft Midwest accent.

'And you have. Tell me all about yourself, Stella. I've rarely felt so much empathy with a Slim-Plicity group leader before.'

(Americans would say that. They are so much more open than us, Stella thought.)

'. . . so much sympathy. I feel we could be very special friends. Come back to my hotel room, and we can talk.'

Stella saw herself with Jo through the eyes of her Heyside group. They would see their Leader, slim and glamorous, talking animatedly to the beautiful Jo McKenzie. They would admire her as she admired Jo.

The car in front of her flashed its amber hazard lights rapidly. Something was wrong. Stella applied the brake gently, and could see that there were road works, and a slalom course to navigate. No matter. She turned on the radio, and music flooded the car. Soon she would be home, talking to Richard – who was arriving back at ten that night – and relaxing and being herself. Her car slowly pushed forward.

Marie turned on Radio Two. It was the King's Singers. She looked out of the window of the lounge down on to the deserted Parade. It was late on Sunday afternoon and the street looked tired, defeated. A thin girl of twelve or so hurried along the pavement, holding a worn cardigan tightly around her. She wore no coat. She was the only person out. Eddies of wind blew stray leaves around, and an empty crisp packet danced with them. Marie was alone. Harry was at the sports club coaching.

It hadn't always been like this. Marie remembered when she was twelve. She was the liveliest one of the family. There were six of them, four boys and two girls, and, true, they were poor, but they knew how to have a good time. When she was twelve Milly was fourteen, but Milly was a bit slow, a heavy, uncertain girl, in type rather like Harry. Marie always felt responsible for her.

When Milly left school and just stayed at home to help in the house, Marie had thought it was because she wasn't fit for anything else. *She* was going to take her matric. But she didn't. She too was made to leave school at fourteen and stay at home. It had been a blow. But she suppressed her anger. Her mother had a weak chest – she needed the help. Her only escape lay in her long conversations with Stan. He was a communist. He hated Mosley. He talked to her about politics. When her parents found out that they were actually courting, they put a stop to it. The family moved to Poplar. Stan took up with someone else. Marie didn't like to think about that time. She met Harry around then. Harry was kind to her, and marrying him seemed like an escape from the intolerable situation at home. He had a stall in the market; it did well, and they bought the shop.

But Harry was a loser. It was only with Marie's determination that the shop conceded them a living.

Harry didn't even talk to her in the evenings. Even in the early years of their marriage he was addicted to those trashy westerns. Sometimes when she spoke to him he didn't respond. So she ate. When she was frustrated, she ate. When she was bored, she ate. When she was angry, she ate.

Stella was meant to change all that. A daughter was something special. In Stella's life she could find fulfilment. But that girl had always pulled away. My God, you can't even talk to her! You say anything, she runs off into her bedroom. So what if she had too many bagels. It's not such a terrible thing. Mind you, they had made up afterwards. They always did. And she was proud of Stella. She had done better for herself than Milly's Rosemary, who was working to pay off her husband's gambling debts. And it was not too late for Stella to have a baby. Who knows? Perhaps she was so moody because she was already pregnant. Marie turned off the radio. It was depressing her. She would ring up Milly, and see how she was. She drew the curtains, and picked up the phone.

CHAPTER NINE

On the table next to the television were a jug kettle, two willow-pattern cups and saucers, and in each cup were sachets of coffee, sugar, miniature tubs of milk (not skimmed) and tea-bags. Two small packets of digestive biscuits sat next to the cups. The rush of cascading water continued. Geoff was having a very thorough shower. Although pleased by this evidence of personal hygiene, Judith was still ill at ease. The hotel was lovely, and their room delightful. The rose-patterned bedspread matched the curtains, and there was a trouser-press. Judith was sorry she hadn't brought any trousers. It would be fun to watch television in bed together. The telephone was also a radio alarm clock. She picked up the maroon folder that contained details of the hotel's catering arrangements, fire regulations, and other leaflets extolling the delights of Hebden Bridge. Judith had only ever driven through here before, and was looking forward to seeing the town in the morning. But there was still the night to come.

Judith rose from the bed where she had been sitting, opened the wardrobe door, and examined herself in the full-length mirror. She was wearing a long satin-effect black skirt, with a brief white blouse that left a small area of flesh exposed above the waistline of the skirt. The result was good; she looked very slim. In accordance with the habit she had recently developed, she pulled in her stomach as far as it would go, and saw with satisfaction how tiny her waist was. With her hair up, and her carefully applied make-up, she could almost see herself on *Dallas*, or *Dynasty*. Her husband, the multi-million dollar oil magnate and reformed alcoholic, was showering in the bathroom, prior to their private dinner with the President. Yet she knew all eyes would be turned on her. Judith was a little worried about dinner, as she did not want to eat too much. Perhaps she would suggest a bar snack.

The water stopped. Judith tensed. He would emerge from the shower in a moment. She hoped he would not try to make love yet. She wasn't quite ready. It was only six o'clock. More than two weeks had elapsed between their decision to stay at a hotel and this long-awaited evening. Geoff had been ill. He had suffered an attack of food poisoning (Emma's cooking, no doubt) and was off work for four days. Luckily he had been able to ring her so she was not too worried. She didn't like to think of him with food poisoning. She would have preferred him to have had flu, which was more romantic. But now he was better, and he had made a reservation at the Benson's Hotel in Hebden Bridge. Len did not seem to care when she said she was going to stay overnight at a friend's house, but then they had hardly seen each other for weeks. Judith knew her marriage was dying, but would not think about it. Geoff opened the bathroom door and stood there, in a white bathrobe, with wet hair. Judith tried not to look at his legs, which were spindly and hairier than Len's. Otherwise he looked good in the bathrobe, like a footballer emerging from a shower after his victory in the FA Cup Final. But it seemed obscene to Judith, Geoff standing there almost naked, and she fully dressed. She quickly reached for her handbag, and took out her packet of St Moritz.

'I shan't look while you get dressed.'

Geoff was perversely aroused by her reluctance. Women ought to be shy about these things. Quite satisfied, Geoff began to dress while Judith stood with her back towards him, smoking her cigarette.

The bar was crowded, but the waiter had neverthe-less found them a small table in a corner. The raucous sounds of a wedding party filtered through from the next room. Judith did not feel guilty at this reminder of matrimony. In the impersonal surroundings of the hotel, she felt divorced from any reality. This was how she liked it. They had not had a bar snack; Geoff had wanted to eat properly (as he said) and they had chosen the table d'hôte menu in the restaurant. Judith had melon, followed by dover sole, and omitted the pud-ding. She watched Geoff eat his pâté, steak and gâteau with enjoyment. They had shared a bottle of wine, and now they were drinking again. Geoff looked wonderful in a jacket and tie. They sat close and Geoff held her hand. People must think they were very elegant. A man was playing a piano in another part of the bar. It was like *Casablanca*. Images of Humphrey Bogart swayed and merged with Geoff. His physique was sim-ilar to Bogart's, even if the hair colour was wrong. She squeezed his hand.

'I'm just going to the Ladies, Geoff. I won't be long.'

'We'll go up to our room when you come back.'

She nodded her assent.

No one else was in the Ladies. Judith looked at herself in the mirror. She was flushed. It must be the wine, she thought. She pulled down her blouse slightly to expose her cleavage. She opened her handbag and took out her packet of pills. As she swallowed the small green pill she reflected that an action that had been so routine and simple was now deliciously wicked. She disappeared into the centre cubicle. When she came out she was still alone. She washed her hands with pink liquid soap from the dispenser. She began to wonder what it would be like, making love to Geoff. The physical side of her marriage with Len had always disappointed her. He was so slow, every move was so drawn out for him. She always had to find something to think about when they were making love. His insubstantial frame moving over hers gave her no real satisfaction. Geoff was much bigger than Len. As she looked in the mirror again she pursed her lips and blew herself a kiss. She had never felt so seductive. As she rubbed her hands under the dryer she became aware of her wedding ring. She took it off.

When she returned to the bar, Geoff was standing up by their table. She wondered what he would be like undressed. Her glance travelled downwards and she looked at the bulge in his trousers. She was shocked at her own audacity. She moved towards him and stumbled slightly. Alcohol always made her unsteady. Geoff took her by the elbow and led her out of the bar.

Once more Geoff was in the *en suite* bathroom. Judith began to take off her clothes, and hung them in the wardrobe; a difficult procedure, as the hangers were fixed. Once she was in her underwear she paused. Not only was she reluctant to be seen entirely naked, but she had bought these frilly black panties and bra especially for this occasion, and she wanted Geoff to see them. She waited. And soon enough the bathroom door opened. And Geoff stood there, in a pair of black pyjamas, with a dragon motif. Judith was delighted with his appearance. But the straight creases betrayed that he too had purchased these for her. She was flattered. He looked so romantic.

'Judith . . . you're so beautiful!'

She felt beautiful, beautiful and sexy. He approached her and they embraced. He began to kiss her neck, and she was aware of the fresh minty smell of his toothpaste. His lips found hers and his kisses became more searching. She could feel his erection pressing against her. It was as if all her warmth, all her sensation, lay between her legs. She had difficulty standing. Geoff stroked her and his hand moved up her thighs. She could stand no longer. As they fell on to the bed Geoff turned out the lights. He lay heavily on top of her, and she was crushed with his weight. She was half suffocated too. But this was what it should be like. He was a real man. And he was about to claim her for his own. She was ready to receive him.

The lovers woke, and embraced once more. Len moved the hair from Emma's face tenderly.

'You're wonderful,' he said.

She clasped him to her. Some time elapsed before they went downstairs into the kitchen to make breakfast. Len watched the toast while Emma popped into the adjoining bathroom for a wash. She had been able to spend the whole night with Len, as Geoff had gone away somewhere. It was wonderful for her to have her lover in her home. She was proud and defiant; she would not mind if Geoff came home and found them there. The past few weeks had been a nightmare, living in the same house with him. They had been sleeping apart, hardly talking. She had kept Len secret only because he belonged so entirely to her. Emma was joyous this morning. Excitement coursed through her. She glimpsed the garden from the bathroom window and saw that it was sunny.

'Len!' she said, as she came out of the bathroom. 'Let's go somewhere this morning. Somewhere open, where we can walk and breathe.'

Suddenly Emma found her own house stifling. The reminders of her old life were niggling her. She needed to be somewhere different, where she could begin again.

'A great idea. I know somewhere . . .'

Within the hour Len was parking the Cavalier near to a television transmitter on a road leading out of Oldham to the M62. The surrounding moorland was bleak and rolling. It was blowy outside the car and they both fastened their jackets against the oncoming wind. Emma was exhilarated.

'This is part of the Pennine Way,' he said. 'We can walk along the border between Lancashire and Yorkshire.'

They skirted the side of the television transmitter and proceeded towards a high narrow foot-bridge that hung precariously across the M62. They crossed it to the deafening roar of cars and lorries passing beneath.

Once on the other side Emma became aware of the springiness of the soil. The peat rose and fell with their footsteps, supporting their strides. Emma imagined she could sense the goodwill of the earth. A new future seemed to be opening out in front of her.

'I owe Liz and Martha a good deal, and I do like them, but I wish this picket wasn't taking place. It's in a fortnight, you know.'

'Surely it's illegal to picket outside a shop.'

'No. I don't see how it can be. This is a free country, a democracy. Everyone has the right to free speech.'

'Do you have to do it with them?'

'Yes, I do. Although I didn't vote for it at the meeting I feel honour-bound to stick by them. And I won't pretend I'm not scared. I think we'll provoke more ridicule than support. It's a misguided idea.'

'Would you like me to be around when it takes place?'

'Yes, I think I would, Len. I'm going to say this because I must. I'd like you to be around all the time. Can we live together? My marriage is over, and yours sounds bad enough. Because . . . I think . . .'

Her voice faltered. She was far more frightened of a negative response from Len than the picket. She had chanced everything. She wanted him badly. His answer was to embrace her. They stood, clinging together for some time. Three hikers, plashing in the marshy soil in heavy boots, approached and saw them.

'Cathy! Heathcliff!' they called.

The lovers came back to consciousness. They smiled.

'Where shall we live?' asked Len. 'Do you want me to move into your house? Or what? How shall we . . .'

'Stop. I don't know. I think the first thing is to tell our partners. For me that's the biggest hurdle. I don't care what Geoff feels, but when he's angry he can be very ugly.'

They came to a large pool of black water. It seemed impassable. Their trainers would let in water. On either side of the bog were tall reeds, suggesting yet more marsh. Clouds scudded across the sky.

'Shall we turn back?' said Len. 'It's chilly up here, and I know somewhere we can get lunch. It's about a half hour's drive. We'll carry on talking somewhere warm.'

With a maternal affection, Judith watched Geoff eat his cooked breakfast. A man needed something hot in the mornings. She had only eaten half a grapefruit and some All-Bran. The aroma of the sausages and bacon tempted her but the knowledge of the calories therein prevented her from eating any.

'What will we do this morning, Geoff? I don't want to stay in the hotel.'

'Shall we go for a walk? See if any shops are open?'

'I'd love that. Tracey at the office says Hebden Bridge is very pretty.'

'And so are you.'

Judith flushed with pleasure. She moved her foot next to his beneath the table. She enjoyed flattery. Geoff was wonderful. He had not disappointed her last night. He had made love with vigour and it was over very quickly. He made love to her again this morning. She must be irresistible, she thought with a glow. A waiter came to remove Geoff's plate.

First they thought they would go down to the canal. They reached it by crossing the main road, and traversing a paved area with benches around it. Judith was quite impressed. On the canal was a barge, and she was keen to have a look at it. Geoff ushered her down some steps to the barge, and she ducked her head and went in. The boat was simply a tourist information centre. A young lady smiled at them from behind a counter and wished them a good morning. Judith picked up some leaflets about canal trips, local walks, clog factories. There was nothing else to do there. They went back up to the street.

They turned their footsteps towards the town centre. Judith was attracted to the displays of fashion in the windows of the numerous dress shops, and Geoff stood politely by. They did not interest him, of course, but he was pleased to see Judith take an interest in such matters. This was more like it. Most of the shops were shut. Then they noticed a small river, over which was a stone bridge. Judith insisted they go to inspect it. She was in fact a little disappointed in Hebden Bridge so far. The stone-built houses seemed poky to her, and the shops were small. But the bridge over the river looked quaint and appealing. They stood there, watching the scene beneath.

Some small children were feeding ducks. The mallards were hungry, and clamoured around the children, some even leaving the water to get as near to the source of food as they could. In the distance some Canada geese were approaching, honking loudly. One little boy, alarmed by the cacophony of sound, was backing away, clutching a crust of bread.

'Did you ever want children, Jude?'

His past tense was interesting.

'I'd love a little boy. But what with saving up, and then waiting while I joined Slim-Plicity, we never did.'

'I wanted a son too.'

Both were silent. They were on dangerous ground. They had not yet spoken about the future. Geoff could not imagine being alone. He had lived with his parents right up until he married Emma, and was used to being looked after. If he was to leave Emma, it would have to be to go to Judith. And she suited him. She agreed with everything he said, she behaved correctly, and didn't criticize his performance in bed. Emma had tried that, once. It would be good to live with Judith. Yet he fought shy of any commitment. It seemed a big step.

A son, Judith thought dreamily. They would have a son, first. Geoff would be rapidly promoted and they would buy a house in Bamford – the very best part of Rochdale. There would be a Sky satellite dish on the roof, a BMW in the drive, and, as Geoff drove up it in the evenings, she would be standing at the window holding up the baby, waving his little fist at his daddy. And lying on the back seat of the car would be a dozen red roses, just for her.

'Geoff. What are we going to do now?'

'Find somewhere to have lunch?'

'No. I mean, about the future. I don't want this to be the last time we're together.'

'It won't be. I love you Jude, you know that.'

'I don't want to return to Len.'

Geoff thought of his loveless home.

'We could live together.'

'Yes.'

Judith kissed him. It was not quite what she wanted, but it was a start. She filled with happiness.

'All right, then. We'll have some lunch. Let's find somewhere warm where we can talk.'

On the right-hand side of the bridge a steep cobbled path led ever upwards; the left-hand side of the bridge led to more shops and civilization. Judith and Geoff chose the left. Shortly they came to a large, inviting gift shop. A board outside announced that coffee and snacks were available inside. The lovers wandered in, their eyes straying to the different displays of decorated coffee mugs, coloured candles, furry toys and tea-cloths with maps of Yorkshire. Judith noticed on the counter a revolving display of ear-rings. She had a weakness for ear-rings and her collection at home flowed out of her jewellery box and on to the dressing-table. The shop was L-shaped, and at the bend Geoff could see the area where food and coffee was served, and he hurried Judith on, past the ear-rings. Near the self-service counter a large menu on the wall revealed what was available.

It was basically pancakes. There was a help-yourself-to-salad display, but clearly the clientele were expected to eat buckwheat pancakes, filled with cheese, or tuna, with God knows how many calories. Judith contemplated skipping lunch and just having a coffee, but she really was very hungry. And perhaps now that she was ten pounds under Bull's-eye it didn't matter for once. Both she and Geoff ordered a buckwheat pancake. They sat down at a round table to await their order.

They had been driving for well over half an hour, and Len had just negotiated successfully a series of alarming hairpin bends which brought them up to yet more bleak exposed moorland. Emma had preferred the countryside lower down, from where it was possible to see the whole valley. As they drove along, a long, low white building became visible, and Len slowed down. This was a pub, known locally as the Ridge, and Len pulled in to the uneven car-park. Some tattered sheep contemplated their arrival.

The interior of the pub was very satisfying. The ceiling was low and the décor subdued. Prints of agricultural machinery and local maps hung on the walls. Len and Emma chose a table near the window overlooking the car-park, and ordered cottage pie and baked potatoes. That was after Len had brought back from the bar a pint of the local bitter for Emma and an orange juice for himself.

Emma felt she did not want to talk about the future here. Sitting companionably with Len in this pub, she wanted to savour the moment. She did not want to talk of Geoff yet. They spoke of their jobs, their childhood.

Then, summoning her resolution, Emma said, 'Perhaps if I left him a note, and gave as a reason that I'd seen him with another woman . . .'

Len listened.

'No!' she exclaimed angrily. 'That's a coward's way of doing it. I'll speak to him tonight, and say that our marriage has broken down irreparably and I've met someone else . . . But what if he turns violent against you?'

They gazed out of the window. It was threatening rain. The sheep had huddled together in a corner.

'Is there anywhere we can go this afternoon, Len? I'm not ready to go home and face him yet.'

'Yes. I know a nice place not far from here.'

Emma looked out of the window of the car and enjoyed the spectacular hilly countryside. The blackened stone cottages along the roadside intrigued her, and she idly wondered what it would be like living here with Len. They would only need a small two-up and two-down. A number of her feminist friends lived in this area, and there was a lot going on. It wasn't a bad idea. Jobs permitting, they could both do with a new start. But she kept her thoughts to herself.

Later, when they arrived in the nearby small town, and they had wandered for some time through its narrow streets, it was hard for her not to share her thoughts with her lover. She was enchanted by Hebden Bridge. So far it had avoided becoming a tourist centre. In its ordinariness it was a place you could imagine living, shopping in. And yet there was something bohemian about it. She had noticed a number of health food shops in among the gift shops; they had stopped to examine some crystals in a New Age craft shop. She had been most encouraged by the number of posters advertising meetings for all sorts of worthy activities: women's groups, yoga, guitar tuition, Greenpeace branches. Never had she been in a place with which she felt so much affinity. Together they walked into yet another craft shop.

★

The buckwheat pancake had been very rich. Judith had an uneasy feeling that she shouldn't have eaten it. It was strange how quickly she could feel insecure about her new figure. She saw a woman paying for food at the counter, accompanied by a small child.

'Geoff. Am I as fat as her?'

'No. You're gorgeous.'

She did not believe him. She was compromised by that pancake. Geoff went to the counter to settle the bill and she rose to join him. Judith thought she may as well go to look at the ear-rings. She would like to have a memento of this weekend.

All of them were very nice. She paid little attention to the wooden parrots, but admired a pair of silver filigree ear-rings. Perhaps they were rather too long. She fingered a pair that were simply spirals of metal. As she tried to pull the next section of the display round to her view, she felt a tension that indicated that the woman next to her was pulling it in the opposite direction. She glanced briefly at the woman, and saw with distaste that she was fat. At least she was not as fat as that. Geoff came over to her and put his hand protectively on her shoulder. Strengthened by his gesture of affection she looked at the woman next to her full in the face.

She felt Geoff clutch her shoulder hard. She did not know why. But when she saw that her husband had his arm round this woman's waist, she reached out to the counter for support. And the four of them were stunned into silence.

CHAPTER TEN

The printing was amateur, but otherwise Liz was perfectly satisfied with the quality of the leaflets. Sandra, her latest recruit, had helped her write them. In the corner of each leaflet was a cartoon of a fat woman sitting slumped in misery surrounded by pencil-thin women parading the latest fashions. The heading was THE FORGOTTEN WOMEN.

'We are the forgotten women,' it ran. 'We have chosen not to starve ourselves into the current fashionable shape, but to simply be ourselves. However, the fashion industry ignores our existence. Chain stores such as Du Mont – and they are not the only ones – stock clothes starting at size eight, and effectively ending at size fourteen, thus omitting to provide for the large section of the population who are size sixteen and over. Have you also experienced the misery of struggling to zip up a skimpily cut skirt, to be told that "we don't normally stock *your* size"? Have you realized that these shops are telling fat women that they are excluded from looking good? They encourage dieting, and dieting can be dangerous.

'Join us! We are a group of fat women who are happy and proud to be ourselves. Throw away your calorie counters. Let your body discover its true shape. Don't shop at Du Mont or chain stores like it. For more information . . .'

Five hundred of these leaflets lay in two piles on

Liz's capacious desk. Lying across the desk, and balanced against the wall, were some placards attached to wooden poles. The first read FIGHT FAT OPPRESSION. That was Martha's. The second was hidden behind the first, but Liz knew that hers said JOIN US IF YOU'RE GLAD TO BE FAT. It had a familiar ring to it, she thought. Emma and Sandra had opted to hand out the leaflets, and as yet she did not know how many of the others would turn out, although she had organized attendance on a rota basis. The picket was to begin at two that afternoon. Liz was excited at the thought of all the publicity they would gain. This translated itself into an overpowering need for food. She went downstairs to the communal kitchen, and made herself two rounds of cheese sandwiches. She consumed them with real enjoyment.

In the distance she heard the doorbell ring. Someone answered it and heavy footsteps made their way across the corridor leading to the kitchen. It was Martha. The toggles on her red duffle-coat were fastened and the material pulled tightly across her. She wore black denims and Doc Martens. She gave Liz a slight smile.

'I'm early, but I've brought the van with me. I think we'd better use that rather than your Beetle, as we can fit the placards in more easily. Remember your gloves: your hands get cold keeping those things upright. There was quite a frost this morning.'

Thirty minutes later two women, one in a red duffle-coat and the other in green oilskins, loaded the Transit van. Liz had put a thermos flask filled with coffee in her large pocket. Martha's face was expressionless as she got into the driver's seat and turned the key in the ignition. Liz sat back with an air of happy expectation.

As usual, Sandra was early. It was the curse of her life. She had such a dread of being late for occasions, that she tended to over-compensate and arrive for interviews, tutorials, parties, way before everybody else. This had become such a habit that she had begun to depend on the time for reflection created by her haste. It was now half past one, and the picket was not due to begin until two o'clock. Market Street was very busy.

Market Street ran along one side of Manchester's notorious Arndale Centre. The centre itself, built of dull yellow tiles, from the outside looking more like a vast public lavatory than a shopping arcade, housed all the city's main chain stores. And so the instant familiarity of the shops flanking Market Street robbed Manchester of any claims to originality or character. There were two entrances to the Arndale Centre itself along the street. It was well known that it was easy to get into the Arndale Centre, but fiendishly difficult to get out. And in between two well-known chain stores, and opposite Oakland tailors, nestled Du Mont.

Sandra stood in front of the window display at Du Mont. She could see immediately that they had chosen the right shop. The mannequins were tall, leggy brunettes, with impossibly thin waists. Sandra reflected that even if the clothes inside did fit you, you would never look as good in them as the models did. That was the first illusion. She was intrigued to see that sharing the window with the arrogant mannequins were two grey metallic figures of men. One was a poor copy of Michelangelo's David, complete with fig leaf. The other was a discus-throwing athlete. Sandra pondered on what it was trying to tell her. That *real* men only liked beautiful, elegant women? Did Du Mont realize that the majority of the ancient Greek male population was gay? Or perhaps they were suggesting that their clothes were classics, not to be confused with the cheaper, more tawdry efforts of shops such as Guys and Dolls, and Sylvia Green. Another illusion. As far as Sandra could see, all the clothes in all the shops looked the same. Inside, many women browsed among the rails of clothes, checking labels for sizes, she thought, acidly.

She decided to walk a little way up Market Street. It really was very crowded. Pairs of teenage girls chatted animatedly. A group of youths in leather jackets idled by the hamburger van. Numerous women pushing buggies with plastic hoods like oxygen tents weaved their way through the crowds. The greasy smell of hot dogs revolted Sandra. An elderly couple, seemingly exhausted by shopping, sat on the bench in front of Du Mont. The man lit a cigarette; his wife stared into the crowds, indifferent. Sandra wondered how they would all react when the demonstration started. She felt some trepidation. When she got as far as Debenham's she decided to turn back. The crowd seemed thicker than ever. She looked in the window of Maxi-Mums, the shop that catered for ladies with fuller figures. Sandra found the delicate euphemism worse than the epithet 'fat'. She had been in Maxi-Mums, once. Although the shop professed to cater for the needs of large women, its fashions were precisely the same as those stocked by the other chain stores, fashions that were conceived with the thinner woman in mind, and thus made fat women look cruelly grotesque.

Next door to Maxi-Mums was Sylvia Green. Sandra couldn't imagine herself wearing any of the clothes in the window. Or perhaps it was that she couldn't imagine herself in a situation where she would need to wear clothes so smart and fashionable. She deliberately dressed down. For parties she liked to wear something outrageous. She thought of Helen too. Helen would never wear aggressively fashionable clothes like that. Housewives wore things that weren't too fussy and were easy to wash. And didn't cost the earth. In fact, when you thought about it, chain stores catered for a very small section of the community, the section with the money. And they exploited the dreams of the rest.

Sandra was beginning to feel in the right mood for the picket. She stood outside Du Mont, and gazed opposite to Oakland, and down the street, her eye taking in shop after shop after shop. It was all about money. Even Slim-Plicity charged fees for meetings despite Stella's zealous emphasis that she cared about all her slimmers. Maybe she didn't make a great deal out of it, but someone must. And yet she did not want to criticize Slim-Plicity too harshly. She had in fact been attending meetings with Helen, and had lost nine pounds. It would have been more had she stuck to the manual correctly, but the discussions she had been having with the Fat Women's Support Group had prevented her from dieting fanatically – she felt obliged to eat the odd bar of chocolate. In fact over the past five weeks she had achieved a gradual weight loss by following the dictates of both groups. Helen had lost a great deal more than her, of course. Sandra was a little envious. Helen had lost nearly a stone, and was looking a lot younger. But she had spoken frankly to Sandra about the cost. There were times when she felt acutely miserable at not being able to eat. She felt a dull resentment whenever her husband ate. Life felt all grey, she said. And yet she spoke of the thrill of being able to get into clothes that had not fitted her for years. The problem was, they were no longer fashionable. And she couldn't afford new ones. Sandra turned once more and looked in the window of Du Mont.

She was certain it must be nearly two o'clock. She walked into the Arndale Centre itself. Seeing an escalator in front of her, she wondered if it was possible to enter Du Mont from upstairs. If it were, it would make it very difficult for just a few of them to blockade the whole shop. Had Liz remembered to check the number of entrances? Tingling with impatience, she made her way outside again. She wished they would hurry. And sure enough, amid the shoppers coming towards her from the covered centre were Liz and Martha, each carrying a placard by her side and a 'Beano' recycled carrierbag containing the leaflets. Already they were creating some interest. Shoppers stood aside to let them pass, craning their necks to try to read the slogans on the placards. Two more members of the group joined them. Sandra did not recall seeing them before.

'I suggest we base ourselves right in front of the entrance,' announced Martha. 'That way we'll attract plenty of attention!'

Sandra was enjoying herself. She was an experienced political canvasser, and enjoyed persuading people. She had helped Mark once to sell the *Socialist Worker* in Market Street, although that was a bit lower down, outside Boots. It felt good to be involved publicly in a feminist cause. She waved enthusiastically at Emma, as she saw her approaching them from the top of the street. More and more bystanders were watching the women.

'Right, sisters,' began Liz. 'This is what I suggest we do. Martha and I will stand here with the two placards and try to talk people out of going into the shop. Emma and Sandra can hand out leaflets – only to women, remember. Sue and Janie, you can support us when necessary. I've got Janice and Debbie arriving at two-thirty. Good luck, everyone.'

The women got into position. By now a group of interested individuals had gathered to watch them, blocking the centre of Market Street. To Sandra it seemed as if she were expected to break into song and dance. Everyone passing turned their heads to try to see what was going on. Sandra ignored them. She began to hand out the leaflets to the females that passed her by.

Some stopped to read them. Others glanced at the contents briefly, smiled, and stuffed the leaflet in their pockets. Some threw them away immediately. A middle-aged gentleman asked Sandra politely for a leaflet, and read it with attention.

'Well, this is a new one on me,' he said. 'Are you from the Green Party?'

'No,' said Sandra. 'We're just a group of women

who don't belong to any political party, but we're against the fashion industry putting pressure on women to become slim.'

The gentleman thought for a moment.

'My wife could do with losing a bit of weight.'

He walked away contemplatively. Sandra continued handing out leaflets. She saw that Martha and Emma had succeeded in attracting four young boys who looked about eleven or twelve. All were dressed in the regulation uniform of trainers, denims and striped quilted anoraks. One was doubled over with laughter. Another was pushing his friend in the direction of Martha. This boy, sporting a painfully short crew cut and developing acne, ran up to her and cried, 'Get 'em off!'

Martha stolidly ignored him. Another of the lads approached her.

'I bet you've got big ones, missis.'

'He says he wants to do it with you.'

The boys laughed until tears ran down their faces, egged on by each other's outrageousness. Martha continued to ignore them, arresting shoppers intent on going into Du Mont. One of the lads came up behind her and pinched her bottom. She turned round immediately but was impeded by her banner. He had gone and rejoined his gang. Martha seemed not to care. Sandra felt hurt and angry on her behalf. It could have just as easily been her they ridiculed.

Sandra noticed that the security guards in Oakland had come out to view them. They pointed and laughed. She glared at them fiercely. They returned her glance with amused interest. A lady dressed in a quilted blue three-quarter-length coat approached Sandra.

'Good for you, love. It's time we fatties took a stand. I'm fed up to the teeth with dieting. When you get to my age you might as well enjoy yourself.'

Sandra could have hugged her. She was used to experiencing these extremes of emotion in political confrontations. All those who opposed you were lifelong enemies; those who gave you messages of support you could have gladly died for. Confrontation polarized everything. Similarly when Sandra saw her leaflet read and kept, she was filled with the zeal of the missionary. Perhaps they were doing some good. For every sarcastic wolf-whistle, one woman may be helped. It was worth it, she thought. She heard two teenage girls comment, 'Fat old tarts. Frustrated, that's their problem.'

Liz pulled Sandra's sleeve. 'How are the leaflets going?'

'I've only got about thirty or so left.'

'Good, because I think we're going to have to change our tactics. Martha and I are having a lot of hassle from some lads, and they're preventing us arguing. But anyway, the picket's not working. The shoppers are just going in through an upstairs entrance. What we're going to have to do is get inside the shop and occupy it.'

'Occupy it! With six of us?'

Sandra's internal alarm bells were ringing. Handing out leaflets was one thing; it was not directly provocative. But occupation? Besides, it was bound to end in defeat. Du Mont was large, and there were plenty of staff. Liz continued.

'Look inside. See the cash desk. There's a shelf

below it where the customers write their cheques. If the six of us sat there we could effectively stop them trading. That would make everyone take notice.'

'But they'll call the police.'

'More publicity for us.'

Emma came over to them, having disposed of all her leaflets.

'We're going inside,' said Liz. 'Over the top.' Emma and Sandra exchanged glances. 'But we'll infiltrate slowly, one by one.'

Sandra entered Du Mont, still undecided in her own mind whether to participate in any further demonstration. To avoid suspicion, she examined some of the skirts and matching blouses hanging on rails in front of her. They were silky and attractive but Sandra could see immediately that their criticisms were justified. All the skirts had tiny waists. She knew from her own experience how humiliating it was to know that none of these clothes fitted you, and that you were therefore excluded from the mass of fashionable women who evidently had figures like ironing boards. She glanced up. Liz and Martha had positioned themselves close to the stairs, and Emma was near the cash desk. Janice and Debbie had arrived too, and were standing at the main doorway, conspiratorially. She could see that Liz's calculations were right. If they all sat on the shelf in front of the cash desk they would cause a considerable obstruction.

'May I help you?'

'I'm just looking,' said Sandra. They've cottoned on, she thought.

And then Liz shouted, 'Now!'

Sandra pushed her way to the cash desk and sat on the shelf beneath it. Martha bumped against her as she hoisted herself up too. The sales staff looked on with consternation. Eight substantial ladies sat in a row, like characters from some obscure nursery rhyme. A slightly balding, middle-aged man, with a distracted mien, hurried downstairs. The manager, no doubt, thought Sandra.

'Please will you get down from there. You are obstructing our business.'

'What have you got to say about your policy of only catering for thin women?'

'I'm here to run a business. Will you kindly get down.'

'Your clothes discriminate against the majority of women.'

'If you don't get down immediately I shall call the police.'

By now Du Mont had filled up, and it contained more customers than it had probably ever done before, or ever would do. The lads who had been tormenting Martha came in too, wolf-whistling. Voices muttered, 'What's going on?' The manager gesticulated frantically to a tall dark girl marooned behind the cash desk, pointing to the phone. She began to dial, casting anxious glances down at the women below her.

The eight women linked arms. Sandra tried not to look at the crowd in front of her. The looks of curiosity and contempt she found more destructive to her morale than the threat of the manager to call the police. She had expected that anyway. But she could see that they were all rapidly turning into objects of derision.

179

'Fancy a chip butty, love?' called out a voice.

A policewoman, with her hat almost masking her eyes, entered the store. She confronted the women.

'You're preventing this trader from carrying out his business. Can I ask you to move on, please?'

'We have the right to express our point of view,' asserted Liz.

The policewoman then addressed her specifically, as the ringleader.

'You've expressed it. You've made your point. Now move along.'

'You're a woman. Don't you think it's scandalous that shops like this only stock the smallest sizes? Girls become obsessed with dieting because of places like this.'

'I'm not here to express an opinion. Please will you move on.'

'Have you any idea of the abuse and insults suffered by fat women everywhere? Du Mont promote this view of us by only . . .'

'If you don't get down immediately I shall call for reinforcements.'

Emma was at the end of a row. A young woman, plump herself, came over to speak to her.

'I agree with you,' she said. 'But this isn't the best way to put your message across.'

'I know,' whispered Emma.

The policewoman consulted with the manager. Shortly three male police officers entered the shop. Emma pulled Sandra's arm.

'Let's go. And tell the others to go too.'

'Right, ladies. You've had your fun. We've got better

180

things to do than see to this sort of prank. Off with you.'

Emma and Sandra wondered how they could leave without losing face. If only the policeman had not been so contemptuous. But the second constable prodded the waist of the first one and said, 'You could do with losing a bit. Too many pies and puddings.'

Emma and Sandra got down from the shelf, and soon only Liz and Martha were left.

'I have to warn you that if you don't remove yourselves immediately we will have no option but to use force.'

Sandra could feel the crowd subtly urging the police on.

Liz wriggled her way down and announced to the crowd, 'See. Even the police oppress fat women!' Oddly, she was triumphant. Martha remained seated on the shelf. Her arms were folded and her expression scornful. Two officers moved over to flank her. The third addressed her.

'All your friends have come down now. We don't want to have to hurt you.'

'I don't believe that. I know all about police brutality.'

'It's because we have to deal with the likes of you.'

'You bastard!'

'Right, men!'

The two constables together lifted Martha, who kicked and struggled violently. She knocked down two rails of clothes. Sandra, watching from outside the shop, felt glad. Martha was deposited outside, in a red quivering heap on the pavement. Liz helped her up.

'Those vicious bastards . . .' muttered Martha. 'Next time I'll . . .'

Sandra heard the phone ringing downstairs.

A voice shouted, 'Sandra! It's for you.'

She ran down the stairs.

'Hello?'

'It's Helen.'

'Oh, I'm so glad to speak to you.'

'Well, how did it go? Are you all right?'

'Yes, fine. What a shambles at the end. I feel so mixed up about it all.'

'Go on. Tell me about it.'

'We handed out leaflets. That was all right. People laughed at us, and especially at Martha. Then Liz suggested we occupy the shop. We blocked off the cash desk, and then the police came and ejected us. Martha wouldn't move, and she got carried out.'

'Was it worth it, do you think?'

'Everyone made us feel as if we were making a fuss about nothing. But you've got to be fat to understand how we feel. God knows what the press will make of it. In a way, we felt a bit like pioneers – the first women to make a stand against any issue – cruise missiles, male violence – are often seen as extremists. But they turn the tide of public opinion. So many things the first feminists fought for we all take for granted now.'

'So you think you've struck the first blow at the clothing industry?'

'No. That's the awful thing. The issue of fat is quite different to all the other issues. The people in the shop weren't angry with us; they just found us funny. It was that I couldn't take. I couldn't stand being the butt of humour. And it made me realize something. What's been upsetting me about my weight is that – the fear of ridicule. I found today very painful; I just hope some good comes out of it.'

'Poor old Sandra. But your friend Emma was right. A public demonstration like this invites ridicule. Don't you think your friends were a little bit ridiculous?'

'Yes! Yes, I do! And I don't know whether that's because they were, or because even I am so infected by the idea that fat is funny that I turned traitor.'

'Don't be so hard on yourself, Sandra. It's over now. I had another reason for ringing too.'

'Yes?'

'It's Katy's fourth birthday on the twenty-fifth of November. We're having a party for her in the afternoon. I'm a little bit short of help, so I wondered . . .'

'I'd love to, Helen. It's years since I've been to a child's birthday party. What do you want me to do?'

'It's up to you. If you come beforehand to help with the sandwiches, and then stay to give me a hand with the kids, it would be more than enough. I'll pay you the usual baby-sitting rate.'

'Oh, no!'

'I'm not letting you come unless you let me pay you.'

'I'm not happy about it.'

'But I insist . . .'

'Mum. Are you sure you're allowed mayonnaise with your tuna salad?'

'Look, Angie. Who's on this diet? Me or you?'

'All right. Keep your hair on.'

Angie came out from the kitchen with two plates for herself and Maureen. The two children were eating sausages and beans on a red plastic table in the corner.

'I heard something interesting on the radio, Mum. Some women occupied Du Mont in the Arndale Centre, saying they didn't make clothes for fat women. The police had to get rid of them.'

'Why don't they go on a diet like me?'

'You make me laugh! You hate dieting. Since you've been at Slim-Plicity there's been no asking you the time of day. Dad said he thought you were going to hit him last night when he walked in with his meat paste sandwich.'

'Well, he shouldn't have smiled.'

'I think these women in Manchester have got a point. I'm in between a fourteen and a sixteen and I don't find much to fit.'

'But everyone knows it's not nice to be fat.'

'I think it's up to the individual. And we all think you're lovely fat.'

'Don't say that or you'll stop me dieting. You're wicked, you are.'

'Don't you agree, though? About these women, I mean.'

'I suppose they have got a point.'

CHAPTER ELEVEN

Helen did not really approve of My Little Pony portable stables but had nevertheless bought one for Katy. She knew her daughter's face would light up when she saw it. Then Helen had popped in to the Early Learning Centre for some washable felt-tip pens, and she had bought a couple of books while she was there. She was now sitting at the dining-room table wrapping these, as the children had gone to bed. She shared Katy's own excitement at her birthday tomorrow, but was taut with nervous energy at the thought of the party. She dreaded children's parties. But Katy had been invited to so many through play group that Helen felt obliged to do the same for her daughter. It seemed to her as if the mothers of Heyside were caught up in some masochistic conspiracy to suffer in turn at regular intervals. The only mothers she had seen enjoy a birthday party were those who had clearly been at the sherry bottle before it had begun.

Helen took the wrapped presents upstairs to hide them in the top of her wardrobe. She took the chair from the dressing-table and stood on it so she could reach to the top. It was some time since she had looked up there. Partly concealed at the very back were a pair of black trousers and a denim skirt. She took them out. She remembered that about eighteen months ago she had wanted a black jacket, but had only been able to buy it as a suit, and the trousers with it had not fitted her at all. Shamefully, she had hidden them. She handled them now with curiosity. The denim skirt was old; she had bought it when she was at the tech, but had so many pleasant memories attached to it that she had never got rid of it. She got down from the chair and closed the bedroom door. She took off her jeans and put on the trousers. They fitted perfectly. In fact the waistband was loose. It was unbelievable. It defied the laws of physics. A few months ago she had not been able to zip them up. She looked in the wardrobe mirror with delight. She took them off and tried on the denim skirt. That fitted too; it was perhaps a little tight but it fitted. She felt as if someone had given her a present. She was intoxicated. She ran downstairs to Tony.

'Look! What do you think?'

'Very nice.'

'Don't you remember this skirt? It fits me again.'

'So it does. Well done.'

She was a tiny bit disappointed at his reaction. He evidently did not share her euphoria. But why should he? She returned upstairs and looked at herself in the mirror for a long time. She could certainly see now that she was slimmer. She had lost eighteen pounds in total. Even her face had a more defined shape. She put on the black trousers again and went downstairs.

'I've never worn these before, Tony.'

'I thought I didn't remember seeing them.'

'I'm ten stone eight now.'

'Good.'

'What do you think? Do I need to lose any more? Stella says my Bull's-eye is ten one. That's another half stone to go.'

'It's up to you. I'm not really bothered.'

You could always count on a man to give excellent advice, she thought, sourly. She was resentful of him. He didn't know how hard it was. She was aware of a constant feeling of hunger. Stella maintained that the manual allowed you plenty to eat, but in reality that was plenty of cabbage, sprouts, cucumber and grapefruit. Helen had bought the Slim-Plicity cookbook, tempted by the appetizing pictures therein. But most of the dishes that looked so appealing were intended for dinner parties. Helen would hardly cook such meals just for herself, and if she was going to invite anyone over for dinner she'd have the decency to cook them something more substantial. So Helen had fallen into a routine of eating dull, worthy foods, and kept going through sheer determination. But inwardly she knew she was nearly at breaking-point. One could only deprive oneself of food for so long. She no longer fantasized about being slim. She was slim – well, quite slim. Now her fantasies were about eating. When she reached Bull's-eye she would treat herself to a Chinese meal with Tony, to a box of chocolates, to an evening of nuts and wine.

But Bull's-eye still seemed such a long way away. She had noticed that recently her weight loss per week had been dropping. She had also read in one of her magazines that dieting lowers the metabolic rate, and so this phenomenon was bound to occur. More work for less results. And yet . . . She looked at herself again in the mirror. There was no doubt about it – she did look good. Friends had begun to comment. Perhaps it was worth it. Slim. She turned the word around in her mind. It was so infinitely desirable, like a precious jewel. And now it was hers. Stella was very pleased with her. She remembered that next Thursday would mark the end of the eight-week period of the autumn promotion. Stella had said that Heyside was in with a chance. She had promised a mystery prize for the best three losers next week in order to spur her members on to greater efforts. It clearly meant a lot to her. There was to be a buffet supper and presentation at the Carlton International Hotel for the successful group.

She returned downstairs, and went into the kitchen to make a hot drink. She opened the cupboard. It was full of food. Crisps, biscuits, fairy cakes, loaves of bread, bottles of cola, and bags of fun-size chocolate bars. Helen quickly shut the door. It was best to keep right away from it. She was conscious of an undefined relationship between her and the food, as it flaunted itself in front of her. She would not think of it.

Instead she would relax. She would read. One of the best things to come out of her dieting was her reading. This had occurred for two reasons. Firstly, by stopping eating to pass the time, she had discovered a number of opportunities in the day to do things for herself. Once Katy was in play group she came home, and rather than eat she would tidy round, do out one room, and then treat herself to half an hour of a book. And now it was books she was reading, not magazines. Her magazines had provided her with pre-digested gobbets of fiction and information, nearly all instantly forgettable. She had read of countless miracle babies, biographies of television stars, and confessions of adultery. But Sandra had pushed her to read properly. Helen had actually read *Great Expectations*. Parts of it she had enjoyed very much; some bits were heavy going. But she had experienced a satisfying sense of achievement at the end. She found she was thinking about the novel a lot. Then Sandra had said that she ought to read books written by women. She had just started a novel called *Martha Quest*. It seemed to be about a girl in Southern Africa who argued with her mother. Helen found it very absorbing. She would read some now, rather than think about tomorrow.

Sandra had made the icing too runny. So when she lifted a teaspoonful to spread it on the fairy cakes it ran down to the bottom in several pink rivulets. Helen came to the rescue with more icing sugar. Then Sandra pressed out circular pictures of Snow White and Disney's Seven Dwarfs from a sheet of rice-paper and stuck them on the middle of each cake. They looked revolting. There were two dozen more to go; Helen had also bought boxes of My Little Pony cakes, in yellow, and Mickey Mouse and Friends, in chocolate.

In front of Helen was an assortment of large plates, one full of fish fingers, one of cocktail sausages, one of hard-boiled eggs, and one piled high with white buttered bread.

'I'll make up the egg mayonnaise if you get started on the fish finger sandwiches.'

'Fish finger sandwiches?!'

'It's a favourite of Katy's. If you slice the fish fingers down the middle rather than across they should fit nicely.'

It was not easy. But it was absorbing. The house

was peaceful as Tony had taken the kids to the park to keep them out of the way. Sandra was having difficulty getting the breadcrumbed crust to adhere to the fish once she had dissected it. But she was not disheartened.

'How are you getting on with *Martha Quest*?'

'It's very interesting,' said Helen, spreading crunchy peanut butter on slices of bread. 'But I can't say I care for Martha or her mother very much.'

'Why? Mrs Quest won't let Martha grow up. I find it terrifying. The mother's like a witch, encouraging Martha to stay at home, doing nothing.'

'I'll start on the egg mayonnaise now. But Martha's quite rude at the beginning, deliberately picking an argument with her mother when a visitor's there.'

'Yes, but it's only Mrs Van Rensburg. How many do you want me to make?'

'You can use all the bread now. In any argument you can't have one person entirely in the right. Surely Martha must be a little to blame?'

'Yes, I see that. Is this the right thickness? It's interesting, isn't it, the mother–daughter relationship.'

'I bet Mrs Quest never gave Martha a My Little Pony stable! You're more analytical than me. But I see what you mean. What time is it?'

'Half past one.'

'We haven't had any lunch! Are you hungry?'

'Not really. Let's get this done.'

Helen showed Sandra how, with the crusts cut off the bread, it was possible to cut the sandwiches into tiny Swiss rolls. It was possible, but very messy. Egg mayonnaise squeezed everywhere. Sandra licked her fingers at the end. She was quite hungry, in fact. She looked around her. The kitchen was full of party food, ready to be taken out into the dining area. Helen was pouring large bags of crisps into glass bowls.

'I sent Tony to Sainsbury's for the party food, and he came back with peanuts too. I think the little ones are still too young for peanuts. They might choke. Let's put them on one side. When the children arrive, you take their coats and the presents and put them upstairs in Katy's bedroom. Tony and I will be the reception committee.'

'Look at the time! There's only an hour to go.'

'And the kids aren't changed yet!'

'Sandra! Someone's at the door. Can you get it? I'm in the bathroom.'

'Hello?'

'Katy Greenwood's?'

'Yes.'

'I'm sorry I'm a bit early, but I thought I wouldn't be able to find the house. In you go, Jennifer. It finishes at five, doesn't it? Bye!'

Sandra was left with a small silent child, sucking her thumb, and clutching a gaily wrapped present.

'Are you Jennifer?'

The child looked with interest at her feet.

'Shall I take the present?'

She relinquished it dully. Katy flew down the stairs.

'Jennifer!'

Katy took her hand and led her into the lounge, where Tony was blowing up balloons. Sandra removed her coat to reveal an old-fashioned pink party dress.

The child wore white tights that sagged. She looked like a bedraggled Christmas tree fairy. She said nothing.

Twenty minutes later the doorbell rang again. Sandra stood at the foot of the stairs and watched Helen greet a mother accompanying a child who stood at the front door and coughed violently.

'He's over the worst of it now,' she said apologetically. 'Put your hand over your mouth, David! Here's my phone number in case he develops a temperature.'

Sandra took his present and removed his duffle-coat. Then three mothers arrived together. Suddenly the house exploded into noise. The four children they brought ran in and jumped up and down in the lounge. It was hard work for Sandra to remove their outdoor clothing. The three mothers stood in the small hallway, talking.

Yet another mother carried her child in her arms.

'This is Abigail. I've never left her by herself at a party before, but Helen said it would be all right.' She passed her over to Sandra. A large tear rolled down the child's face.

'I'm Rebecca,' announced another little girl, with two beribboned bunches on the top of her head. She tugged at Sandra's shirt.

Helen was speaking to the mothers. She turned round to ask Sandra, 'Where's Katy?'

Apparently nowhere. Shortly Tony found her, hiding in an upstairs bedroom.

'It's too noisy,' she said, as he carried her down-stairs.

And she was right. It was too noisy. All the children

had now arrived, including Matthew's friend Danny. Danny began to dive-bomb the settee, and all the boys followed him. The girls ran round and round the room joyously, shouting and whooping. It was deafening. Outside in the hall the three mothers who had arrived earlier were still chatting, oblivious of the noise. Clearly they had not seen each other for a long time. Helen wished they would go. It was bad enough opening your house to a dozen or so kids, but when it's also used as a general meeting place . . .

It was essential to restore order in the lounge.

Tony cried, 'Who wants to play pass the parcel?'

Sandra watched the children form themselves into an amoeba-like shape on the floor.

'I want to win,' announced Rebecca.

Helen brought in a bulky, newspaper-wrapped parcel from the kitchen, and handed it to a pretty Asian child. She immediately began to unwrap it.

'No, not yet,' said Tony kindly. 'When the music stops.'

The girl was clearly baffled, for as yet no music had started. She fixed Tony with her large dark eyes, and continued to unwrap the parcel. The other children watched her with attention, waiting to see what was inside.

'Put on some music, someone!'

Matthew rushed over to the hi-fi. It was an unmissable opportunity. He knew how to work it. He turned the volume up as high as it would go. The children screamed.

'Matthew! Sit down! I didn't mean you!'

Helen turned down the volume. Half the parcel was

unwrapped, but the girl passed it over with little fuss to the next boy, who proceeded to unwrap it further, to the tune of 'Who's Afraid of the Big Bad Wolf?'

Danny was not playing. He was jumping up and down on the settee now, in time to the music, occasionally precipitating himself off the edge, making a noise like an aeroplane with engine failure.

'You can keep the prize, Rebecca. Now we'll play musical bumps.'

Helen saw that the children were utterly confused. Perhaps it was a mistake to ask Tony to organize the games. He didn't seem to realize how little three and four-year-olds understood. Numb with tension, she turned her back on the maelstrom behind her and looked out of the window. She noticed Judith's front door open. She hoped she wasn't coming across to complain about the noise. But it was Len. He was carrying two large suitcases. Helen did not know that they were going on holiday. Normally they would have asked her and Tony to look after the keys. Len put the cases in the boot of the Cavalier, and returned to the house. This time he came out with some boxes. Helen was mystified. She then remembered Emma. Surely he couldn't be leaving Judith? He must be! Poor Judith! Helen felt as if she ought to go round there and see if she was all right. But the party! Perhaps it would be better to wait until five o'clock. She watched Len drive off alone. There was no sign of Judith.

'No, Jennifer. You've been out once so you can't join in again. Sit with Sandra. MATTHEW! LEAVE THE HI-FI ALONE!'

Abigail burst into tears. 'I want my mummy.'

Helen scooped her up and shot an anxious glance at Sandra. Sandra could see the problem. Tony's party games were beyond the comprehension of the children. She took a deep breath.

'I'm going to play "The Farmer's in His Den". Who wants to join me?'

Reassured by a familiar play group routine, the children formed a circle with Sandra. She led them round slowly. Tony and Helen looked on with admiration.

'Can we do "Ring of Roses", Sander?' asked Katy.

They did.

Then Sandra said, 'Who would like to hear a story?'

'Me! Me!'

'Well, all sit down on the floor. I'm going to tell you the story of Goldilocks and the Three Bears, and you must be very quiet, because I might make a mistake. And if I do you can shout as loud as you like to tell me what I should have said.

'Once upon a time there were three bears. They lived in a cottage in the woods. For breakfast the bears liked to eat Weetabix.'

'No! No! Porridge!' they screamed excitedly. Helen's tension ebbed. She had grown very fond of Sandra, but she had never loved her as she did right now. She turned to the dining-room table to remove the serviettes covering the food. The children would need to eat soon.

The waxen paper plates with their Thomas the Tank Engine motifs were a concession to Matthew, who had threatened to boycott the party because he thought it would be 'soppy'. On each plate Helen had put three small sandwiches, one fairy cake, a handful of crisps and a cocktail sausage. The rest of the food lay in bowls in the centre of the table. The ill-matching chairs had been taken from all over the house. Helen went into the kitchen and returned with a jug of orange squash with which she filled the paper cups on the table. The doorbell rang.

Was it Judith? Helen acknowledged that she wanted it to be. She was wild with curiosity and detested herself for it. She hurried to the door and opened it.

Standing in front of her was a very tall man of cadaverous appearance. His greying hair was thin and scanty; he wore a baggy suit that had seen better days; his look conveyed ineffable sadness. Helen stood there completely at a loss. But the large stiff-sided suitcase reminded her who he must be. Tony's friend Gordon. The magician.

Tony had said that Gordon's hobby was magic, and that he would perform a few tricks for Katy's party. They had arranged for him to entertain after tea, while Helen and Sandra cut the cake and prepared the party bags. Somehow Helen had imagined that he would be much younger. She ushered him into the kitchen.

The children were seated contentedly around the table. The two older boys ate with gusto; the younger children looked suspiciously at the food, as if it might do them some unspecified harm. Each ate the fairy cake first. The sandwiches were bitten into and left. The children were slow, abstracted, as they munched crisps, sipped drinks, and picked the icing off cakes. Helen relaxed. She was beginning to feel hungry.

In order to remove herself from the temptation of the party food, she moved over to the window again, and looked out on to the street. A car pulled up in front of the house: a blue Fiesta. A youngish, sandy-haired man emerged, carrying a suitcase, and walked up Judith's drive. Helen was mesmerized. She watched Judith come out of the house and embrace him. Together they returned to the house with more suitcases.

'Helen, is there any more orange squash?'

Helen swivelled round to find Sandra standing behind her with an empty jug.

'Yes, I'm sorry. But I've just seen something incredible . . .'

Gordon had begun his show. Tony had set up for him a small trestle-table and had covered it with a green velvet cloth. The magician stood behind it, glaring balefully at the children.

'Welcome to the world of magic,' he announced, darkly. 'You see before you a single white handkerchief. I will put this handkerchief –'

A child stood up.

'Sit down, little girl.'

She did, and put her hand up. Her face quivered.

'I need a . . .'

'Be quiet now, or you'll miss the magic.'

A tear rolled down her face. Katy, sitting next to her, interpreted.

'She needs a wee-wee.'

The magician regarded her helplessly. Tony, who was watching, moved over to extract the girl. Meanwhile, Helen and Sandra were in the kitchen, cutting the birthday cake. It was a tricky job. As the knife cut into the cake, the pink icing caved in and flaked off the sponge. Absent-mindedly Helen picked up some icing and put it in her mouth. It melted quickly and filled her mouth with sweetness. It felt such a long time since she had anything sweet. Hoping Sandra wasn't watching, she took some more. The sweetness was cloying. She stopped.

The dozen party bags were propped up on the work surface in the kitchen. Each contained a pad and pencil, two fun-size chocolate bars, a balloon and a slice of cake wrapped up in a serviette. The two women looked at them, satisfied. They could hear gales of laughter from the lounge and frenzied cries of 'Sit down, sit down!'

'They've left a lot of food, haven't they?' questioned Sandra.

'Yes. I've bought too much as usual. God knows what I'm going to do with it all. The children will be living on crisps and sandwiches.'

There was a pause.

'Actually, Helen, I'm quite hungry.'

'Of course. We've had no lunch. Help yourself!'

Sandra took a handful of crisps. She thought she would only have a few, and then ask Helen for a cup of tea and an apple. Helen decided that one fun-size Mars bar would not do her very much harm. Sandra took some more crisps; it was interesting how, as each mouthful was completed, it set up a craving for more.

'I'll have some crisps too,' said Helen.

She plunged her hand into the bowl. She was only conscious of her hunger and a driving need to eat, stronger than she had ever experienced before. Nothing mattered except her and the crisps. All conversation had stopped. Rhythmically, in turn, each woman took a handful of crisps. The pace increased. Helen needed larger and larger mouthfuls. Sandra wiped her hand around the empty bowl, and licked the salt from her fingers.

'We may as well try the birthday cake,' said Helen, feeling an electrifying dissipated guilt, as if she had made an obscene suggestion. Sandra cut two generous slices from the heart on the Care Bear cake. They did not bother with plates. Helen turned to put the kettle on. The noise from the lounge increased. When Tony came into the kitchen neither woman could look at him directly.

'Gordon's nearly finished, but it's only quarter to five. The children are restless.'

When Helen entered the lounge Gordon was already packing up, with a slow concentration, oblivious of the chaos around him. Getting him was another mistake, thought Helen. Once again the children began to chase each other. The whooping and screaming reminded Helen of the swimming baths on a crowded afternoon. She was hot and buzzing with a manic nervous energy. Clearly the sugar had got into her bloodstream.

After an eternity, the doorbell rang, and the first parent appeared. Coats were collected, goodbyes were said, and Helen was assailed by several children mumbling thank you. She saw them off with relief.

She returned to the lounge, where Matthew and Katy were fighting. Gordon was slumped in an armchair, staring ahead of him in a daze. Tony had his back to her, pouring out large sherries for all of them.

One sherry was enough to make both Sandra and

Helen very heady. Back in the kitchen, as they tidied up, their inhibitions were gone.

'Shall we finish off these biscuits?'

'Yes. And open the peanuts while you're at it. We'd better get rid of them. Tony! Why don't we get a Chinese tonight and treat Sandra? She's been wonderful. Here, Sandra. Finish off these egg mayonnaise. I'll help you.'

Helen went upstairs to bring down Katy's presents. In her bedroom she paused. What on earth had she done? For the past hour she hadn't stopped eating. She froze in horror. For that matter, neither had Sandra. That cheered her up. Her heart began to beat again, as she reflected that she had been under a lot of pressure today, of course she couldn't be expected to diet. And why not make a night of it. She could always start again on the manual tomorrow. And it was so unspeakably wonderful to eat unrestrainedly again. Just for tonight. She looked at the parcels on the bed and wondered what could be inside them. Fried chicken in black bean sauce and some sweet and sour pork. She was riotously happy.

CHAPTER TWELVE

Maureen fumbled in her handbag and found Angie's shopping list. There weren't too many items; in fact, the main reason she was at the supermarket for them both was the nappies. Angie had run short of disposables. Kelly still needed a nappy at night-time, and Jason wasn't dry yet. She'd save a lot of money with terries, thought Maureen, and it wasn't as though her daughter didn't have a washing-machine. In her day the things had to be soaked, and boiled, and hung out to dry. Maureen could remember winters when she brought nappies in from the garden stiff as boards. Angie didn't know she was born. That must have been over twenty years ago. Maureen remembered that her fiftieth birthday was only eleven days off. The oddest thing about getting older was that you never actually felt any older inside. True, your body didn't function quite as well as it used to, but Maureen felt that she was the same Maureen she had ever been. But no, she would not let herself get depressed! There was also to be a party at the Wellington for her, and she had lost nineteen pounds so far.

She stretched to take some baked beans from the shelf, and made herself feel thinner. She had actually done very well. She had her moments, when the temptation to eat was just too strong, but by and large she had stuck to it. This weekend she and Angie were going to buy new dresses. After her birthday Maureen's intentions were vague; of course she would carry on to Bull's-eye, as she had done so well; but then there was Christmas, and the New Year. She would not think about it yet. She consulted Angie's list again.

Fancy asking her to get crumpets, when she knew they weren't in the manual, and Maureen liked them so much. The cheek of it! With disdain Maureen dropped them into the trolley. To Maureen, being slimmer and not eating had no real connection. Sometimes she thought about being slimmer, and relished the comments that the other women in the kitchens made about it. But most of the time she thought about not being able to eat. Her decreasing waistline was something that had happened almost by magic; she had forgotten that it was her choice to join Slim-Plicity, and her diet seemed to her as something imposed on her by authority. To her, Stella was indistinguishable from Sister Alban at St Ursula's, the convent school she had attended as a girl. There was never any question that Sister Alban was right. But Maureen didn't always want to do what she was told. And she didn't always do as she was told! She smiled with the remembrance of it. And she always repented heartily afterwards. She was now a good Catholic, and counted it as a personal failure that her son should be living with a girl and not be thinking of marriage.

But she had rebelled against Sister Alban at fourteen, and now there was Stella. Stella to her was a disembodied presence hovering among the shelves in the supermarket: 'Thou shalt not eat *that*; *those* are not in the manual.' And Maureen had to fight hard against the desire to rebel. Sometimes the pressure was unendurable. And she loved food so much.

The supermarket was already full of Christmas provisions. Paper chains hung in festoons from the ceiling; at the end of each aisle were jars of mincemeat and boxes of Christmas crackers. Maureen's bitterness at not being able to eat swelled steadily. And then, at the top of the aisle in front of the bakery was a table laid out with Christmas cakes. Next to the stack of cakes were several trays, holding sample bites of the cake. Maureen deserted her trolley. She moved over to the table to try a piece. It was delicious. She looked about her swiftly. She could see no one she knew, nor were any of the assistants in view. She helped herself to another piece, trying to look uncertain; as if perhaps one more bite would help her decide whether to purchase. She took another morsel. She was joined by a woman who also tried some. Maureen realized she had to stop. Two small children came up. She chose the largest piece left, swallowed it guiltily without pausing to taste it, and went back to her trolley. There were the two packs of nappies on top. Keen to avoid detection, she completed her purchases as swiftly as she could. But inside she felt righteous. If anyone deserved a bit of Christmas cake, it was her. And it was put there for anyone to try, wasn't it? She came to the greengrocery section and bought some apples and a cucumber. At last she had finished.

The check-outs were not particularly busy. Only one elderly gentleman was in front of her, with no more than a basket of items. Angie was right; it was easier for Maureen to go shopping, as she didn't have to take the kids with her, and she could go straight from work in the early afternoon. It was good of Angie to give her money for the taxi. Maureen began to unload the contents of the trolley on to the conveyor belt.

Apples, a cucumber, fish fingers, several tins, two cumbersome packs of nappies, a fresh cream gâteau, four chocolate eclairs, a box of Danish biscuits, a box of Terry's All Gold. What was this? A gift from heaven? A miracle? Maureen continued to unload, in a trance. A tub of large peanuts, packets of Californian corn chips and tortilla chips, cashew nuts. A litre bottle of whisky, a litre bottle of vodka. She was dreaming. It was wonderful. And then she caught sight of the price of the gin she was lifting out of the trolley. She froze. What was going on? What was she doing? She thought she might have a hot flush coming on. This wasn't her trolley.

'You'll have to stop,' she said to the cashier. 'I think there's been a mistake.'

Further down the line of check-outs she could see the manager in conference with another cashier and the woman who had come up when Maureen had tasted the cake. She then realized what must have happened. She must have taken that woman's trolley on returning to her shopping. She was so absent-minded these days; it must be the effect of the diet. As the woman and the manager approached them Maureen saw that this woman was quite slim. How dare she! How could she buy all that food and remain so slim! It wasn't fair. The woman was smiling apologetically, but Maureen had to work hard to control her anger and bitterness. It just wasn't fair!

*

It was only half past six when Stella arrived at the British Legion, but she could not have stayed at home any longer. Everything was reaching a climax. From tonight's figures she would be able to calculate the average weight loss of her Heyside group over the past eight weeks, and would be able to tell if they were in with a chance. They were far and away the best group she led. Not only that, but she had received a letter this morning informing her that she had been selected for interview for the post of Area Co-ordinator, and that the interview would be on the day after the buffet. As yet, of course, she did not know if she would be attending the buffet as the successful group leader. But if she did, and met Jo McKenzie, and then had the interview next day, and landed the job . . . She was giddy with anticipated delight. Stop it! she told herself. None of this may come to pass. And rather than indulge in pointless fantasy at this stage, she decided to set up shop early at the Legion.

The keys were unwieldy, but she eventually gained entrance. The familiar dank smell mixed with stale cigarette smoke assailed her. The room flooded with light. And as she moved around, shifting tables, opening her brief-case, her thoughts returned to their familiar track.

'How wonderful to meet you, Stella. What an excellent average your class achieved. You must be a gifted leader.'

'I've only followed your example, Jo.'

'Maybe. But we all know that you must be someone special. I hear you're being interviewed for Area Co-ordinator tomorrow. It must be important to you.'

'It is.'

Stella was allowed to keep her scales in a locked cupboard in the bar area of the Legion. She took them out now and set them up. She stepped on them herself. Eight eleven. Wonderful! Better than she had hoped. Of course, she had put herself in first gear for all the past week, mainly through superstition. She felt that if she had a good week, her Heyside slimmers would. And she had informed them of her intentions. Perhaps it would spur them on. She wondered how much they thought of her during the week.

On the table by the scales she brought out a clip-board with a sheet of paper attached to it by a bulldog clip. On here Stella had written each group member's total weight lost for the last seven weeks, so that she could add immediately the weight they had lost to-night, and divide it by eight. There might be a chance that Anne would ring tonight and they could compare notes. As far as she could work out, it was between them. But Liverpool and Preston were also included in the north-west. Stella gripped the edge of the table hard. It must, it must be Heyside.

Stella moved to the door in order to wedge it open. She saw her clerks arriving. She greeted them cheerily. It was going to be a good night.

While Mrs Garwood fumbled with her coat, Stella looked down her list of figures. A total of sixteen pounds lost in two weeks meant an average loss of two pounds. And yet several slimmers had lost more than that. Maureen Evans, for example, had lost nineteen so far. Good old Maureen. Stella loved her. And now Elsie Garwood had taken off four! They were bound to do it, bound to win.

(Here's Sandra Coverdale.)

'You've stayed the same this week, dear. Any reason?'

'I wasn't too good on Sunday.'

'Never mind. There's always next week.'

(And why couldn't she have waited till next week! Here's Maureen. She certainly is looking slimmer.)

'That's another three. Well done, Maureen! This is terrific!'

(You can always rely on the old ladies. They're much steadier. Helen Greenwood. She's a good loser.)

'Just a half off this week, Helen. Still, a half's a half.'

'Well, it was what I expected. I wasn't too good on Sunday.'

The last group member had been weighed. With alacrity Stella passed her clipboard to her clerks for an announcement of the figures. She passed them her calculator too. There were to be no mistakes. She thought that anything over two point three would be hopeful. She strode to the front of the class.

'I had a dream. I used to dream that I would be slim. How many of you share that dream? That dream is the one thing that unites us. We are all of different ages, different races, different personalities. But the one thing we have in common is that we all dream about being slim.

'Imagine the day when you look in a full-length mirror and see that the slim lady looking back at you is YOU. Imagine putting on a belt, and discovering that even the tightest notch is too large. Imagine attracting wolf-whistles as you walk down the street. Yes, even you, Maureen. And I am sure that each one of you has your own special dream about being slim. There is one particular reason you are slimming, or perhaps one situation you can see yourself in, slim. Think of it for a moment. And it will come true.

'And yet thinking isn't enough. Slimness is a dream you must work at. Getting slim is a slow, sometimes difficult, process. And we all know, it takes effort. People will dissuade you, your hunger will betray you. But stick with it. Dreams can come true, but only for the determined. My dream of being slim came true; I have other dreams too. I dream that all of you sitting here will be as slim as me, and I know that together we can do it.'

This is one of the best talks I've ever given, Stella thought. If only Jo could hear this.

Just then one of the clerks gave Stella the final figures. She glanced at them, and smiled.

'2.6!'

The group waited for an explanation.

'Your average weight loss over the past eight weeks has been just over two and a half pounds. It might just be enough to make us the best group in the north-west. I shall find out during the week, and let you know at the next meeting. Now, into your Buddy groups.'

There was the familiar shifting of chairs.

'This week, I want you to share your dreams. Tell each other what being slim will mean to YOU.'

Maureen, Helen and Sandra faced each other. Judith had not turned up that week, much to Helen's disappointment. She had not seen her since Sunday. Maureen began.

'Wearing nice clothes, and everybody commenting. That's being slim. That, and not wanting to eat much.'

'When I'm slim,' said Sandra, 'everybody will respect me, and I'll have poise and confidence. I'll be strong and decisive, and I won't keep changing my mind.'

'But you can be those things now, Sandra,' suggested Helen. 'You've every reason to feel confident. You're clever and pretty and beginning your life. I respect you. Look how you charmed the kids at the party.'

'Stella's right. I do dream of being slim. I just feel I could be totally happy if I were slim. If I were slim, nothing would ever bother me.'

Maureen nodded. This was right. Helen broke in.

'Look, Sandra. I'm slimmer now. And I'm no happier. Apart from moments of vanity in front of the mirror, it's changed nothing. I don't think I want to be slim.'

Sandra watched, puzzled, as Helen's face closed and she sensed her friend was repressing something. Sandra felt an instinctive concern, a desire to help. But this was not the place.

'Are you in tomorrow afternoon, Helen?'

'Of course. But Katy only does the morning at play group.'

'I've got a tutorial in the morning. But I'm coming round after lunch.'

The recreation ground was almost deserted. One small

boy scrambled up the climbing-frame, watched by an anxious mother. It was a cold afternoon. The sky was a brilliant blue, but without warmth. The illusion of summer was there, but the bitter reality was winter. At least it was not raining. That meant, with sufficient outdoor clothing, Katy could be taken to play on the swings and slide. She was wearing a pink quilted jacket, mittens, and a grey balaclava of Matthew's that was now too small for him. Helen thought she looked like a little refugee. But Katy was perfectly content. She was going to the park with Sandra and Mummy. This was how it should be.

Helen lifted her daughter into a black rubber baby swing, and Katy held on to the top bar. Helen pushed from the front, watching Katy's eyes and sharing her pleasure as she swung higher and higher. Her cheeks reddened with the cold, and a stream of mucus ran from one nostril. Helen stopped pushing the swing to feel in the pocket of her anorak for a tissue.

'More! More!'

Helen resumed pushing. As her arms accustomed themselves to the rhythm of the swing, her mind was freed. She wondered what Sandra must think, standing there by the end of the row of swings, watching her. It was a little undignified, pushing a child in a swing. And the relentless need to push, and then to push, and then to push, caught Helen up in an intimacy with the swing and the child that excluded Sandra. When the children were very small it was an intense pleasure to place them in a swing, and watch their baby faces move from uncertainty to wonder, to excitement. But now in Katy's face was smug certainty. Mothers existed to push little girls in swings. She felt, rather than knew, that her daughter denied her individuality, loved her for what she did for her, not for what she was. And that heavy depression that had been with her since Sunday came back in full force.

Sandra approached her.

'Here. Let me take over.'

'No. It's all right. She'll be out in a minute and wanting the slide.'

At the mention of the slide, Katy was already trying to scramble out of the swing. Helen held it steady and lifted her out. The two women watched her run over to a small painted slide, climb up the three steps, and come down the other side, slowly, as she would not lift her feet up. Helen and Sandra sat down on a nearby bench.

'Do you come to the park a lot, Helen?'

'Most days.'

Helen seemed uncommunicative. Katy came rushing over.

'I'm going on the climbing-frame! Watch me!'

Both women did.

'Helen, what did you mean last night when you said you didn't know whether you wanted to be slim? I thought you were keen on Slim-Plicity. Keener than me.'

'Well, what's the point?'

'Feeling good, I suppose. Achieving something. I mean, if that's the target you set yourself. But it wasn't just what you said; it was the way that you said it. You seemed – I don't know – as if you had given up.'

'Look at me! You're not watching!'

'Clever girl, Katy. I suppose I have.'

'It wasn't that binge at Katy's birthday, was it? I binged too; I probably had more than you. It was me who finished off the chow mein, remember, and that's loaded with calories.'

'Help me. I'm stuck!'

Helen rose from the bench and moved over to her daughter and lifted her down from the climbing-frame.

'Go and play on the rocks.'

At one end of the recreation area were some large rocks scattered over a small area. Helen could never decide whether they had been put there on purpose by the Parks Department, or whether some benign deity had dropped them there for the gratification of the infants of Heyside. The children loved to jump on and off them; they played ships, chasing games, had picnics. Katy was now perfectly content skipping on and off the rocks, lost in a game of her own devising.

Helen wanted to talk.

'It began with the binge. No it didn't. It was before. The night before the party. I tried on some old clothes. They fitted. I was elated. But that night I couldn't fall asleep; I suppose I was tense about the party. Then the thought of the clothes made me very depressed. I felt so much older, as if all the fun had gone out of life. Even if I wore that denim skirt again, everything would be different. I wouldn't be at the tech with the girls. I'd be a housewife and mother. I felt as if my life was over. I wondered if dieting was just a way to put back some of the old excitement.

'Then there was the binge. Sandra, I've never eaten so much in my life. After you went, I carried on. I thought I might as well have some ice-cream – I don't even like ice-cream! – and I carried on after that. All night long I was uncomfortable. Then when I woke up in the morning my body hurt.'

'I used to do that before I joined Slim-Plicity and the Fat Women's Support Group. I did it whenever I thought of going on a diet.'

'Then I thought, if I hadn't been dieting, I wouldn't have been bingeing. In the morning I hated myself. I felt as if I deserved some sort of awful punishment, something that really hurt.'

'I know! That's just how I felt.'

'And what's the point of being slim, if you're constantly struggling to keep yourself that way?'

'That's why I joined the Fat Women's Support Group. I wanted to escape that cycle of overeating and punishment. You really ought to come to a meeting with me, Helen.'

'No. I can't see myself in a picket. It's not me. But Sandra, something else happened too. It wasn't just the binge.'

'Tell me.'

'It's hard to explain. It doesn't matter.'

'I'll understand.'

'No, I don't think I want to talk about it.'

Sandra knew never to force a confidence. And she did not want to appear curious. But the will to help her friend was strong in her. Silently she urged Helen to talk. Both women watched Katy moving from rock to rock. In the far distance they could hear an ambulance siren. Then all was still.

'Oh, I suppose it's nothing really. Just like me to

make a mountain out of a molehill. I'll tell you. On Sunday Tony said, since the business was doing so well, why don't we try for another.'

'Business?'

'No, baby.'

'Don't you want one?' Sandra deliberately spoke neutrally.

'No. When he said it, it was like someone had put tight bands round my chest. I panicked.'

'Surely he wouldn't insist. Tony seems so good-natured.'

'Of course he didn't insist. He just said he thought I'd been looking a bit fed up lately and it would give me something to do. And that was what really upset me. Even to him I was a non-person – just there for kids. And I began to realize why I'd resented him so much lately. I thought it was because I was bad-tempered on the diet. And I'm sure I was sometimes. But little things he would do, annoyed me. He would leave the milk-bottle tops off the milk bottles. I'd swear under my breath. Or when he left the newspaper by the side of his armchair. He never picks it up.'

'Typical of men,' said Sandra evenly.

'Yes; and I should let it wash over me. But I can't. Oh, this sounds so awful. I do love him, and I can't even put into words what I feel about the children. Let's admit it, Sandra; I'm also jealous of you.'

'Of me?'

'You've got no responsibilities; you do something interesting every day. No, this is ridiculous. It's just my mood – probably premenstrual tension or something. Forget everything I said.'

Sandra was silent.

'All I mean is, I've been dieting; I've lost quite a lot of weight. I thought someone would notice me, and see me properly. But nothing's changed. And why should it? I know they all love me. I ate before through boredom, but I'm still bored. I might as well eat; I've got nothing else to do.'

Her voice trailed away. But Sandra was thinking.

'That's not true. You've been reading. You enjoyed *Great Expectations*. And I can have more intelligent discussions with you than with lots of my friends. Look how you just analysed how you were thinking. That was great. Have you thought of going back to education, Helen?'

'I'm too old.'

'Nonsense! All the universities take mature students now. There's a couple on my course.'

'But I've only got five O-levels. Don't be ridiculous. I don't know the first thing about studying. And where would I find the time?'

Sandra was enjoying herself. It was exciting to be helping someone else. For once she felt sure of her ground.

'These days universities waive formal entry requirements for mature students, that is, provided you can show some sort of competence. And you can't say you don't have the time, because you're sitting here and telling me you're bored.'

'It's no good, Sandra. I appreciate what you're saying, but I don't really have the confidence. I've been at home with the children for years. I'm used to it. I couldn't change now.'

'Coward!'

'No, I'm just realistic.'

Katy returned to them. She hugged her mother's legs and put her head on her mother's lap. The balaclava slewed to one side, and gently Helen moved it back. She stroked her face.

'Shall we go home and have something nice for tea?'

'Not yet,' said Sandra. 'Come here, Katy.'

She took the child on her lap and held her firmly.

'I've heard about special courses, "New Opportunities for Women", I think they're called. I've seen them advertised. They're for women who want to start over again. Some local authorities run them. Part of the course is designed to build your confidence, and part is academic too – I mean you can read and study literature, or maybe learn to operate a computer. But it will start you off. At the most it would be for a day a week. And usually these things are run to suit mothers with small children; they're in school hours. Why don't you find out more about them. Try the library.'

'What? You mean like an evening class?'

'Yes, but in the afternoon. Or the morning.'

Now Helen was silent. Then she said, 'With other women like me?'

'Yes.'

Helen imagined what it would be like, learning again. Something roused in her. She wanted Sandra to go on talking about it.

'Does it cost a lot?'

'Very little. These things are subsidized.'

Helen's interest was awakened. She was beginning to feel quite different. When she had started Slim-

Plicity, she had done so in a mood of self-disgust. But this time she was being made to consider her own potential, her own strengths. Sandra had said she was analytical. What if she did make something of herself? And this time she wouldn't be working on her body shape, but all of her . . .

'Come here, Katy.'

The child slid off Sandra's lap and clambered on to her mother. Helen sat her astride her legs and bounced her up and down, much to the girl's delight. Helen's spirits lifted.

'How would you like it if Mummy went back to school?'

'Nice.'

The three of them walked back from the park. Katy walked in the middle, and was occasionally swung laughing into the air.

'Well, Sandra, what shall I do about Slim-Plicity? I feel bad about just dropping it.'

'Look – I'm going back home for Christmas next Friday. Next Thursday would be my last meeting anyway. Why don't we go and get weighed? It'll give us a chance to make up for our binge, and you can tell Stella that it's not for you.'

'What will you do, Sandra?'

'I don't know yet. I'm absolutely convinced that fat women are badly treated. But I can't rid myself of the desire to be slim. I think fat *is* a feminist issue.'

'But why should it be an issue at all? Look at us, constantly worrying about our weight, what we eat . . . Aren't we ridiculous?'

'Yes, I suppose we are.'

They quickened their pace with Katy between them. She tensed her arms in preparation.

'One . . . two . . . three . . . Wheeee!'

CHAPTER THIRTEEN

She fingered the pendant, and cradled it in her hand. She had never seen anything quite like it. The chain was silver, and suspended from it was a crumpled silver leaf, and nestling within that was a crystal, which fired with many colours as Stella shifted it in the light. She loved it. It sparkled at her, and she felt it had caught her mood perfectly, for she was ecstatic. She had won. They had won. Early that afternoon Deborah had smilingly informed her that Heyside's average weight loss was the highest in the area, narrowly beating Liverpool by two tenths of a pound. She had proved she was the best. And she would have dinner with Jo McKenzie.

Should she buy the pendant? True, it was expensive, but money was not a problem, and how lovely to have something to remember this moment by. She had never felt quite so alive as now. She needed to jump, or run along the street with the abandon of a child, if she were to express herself fully. But that was ridiculous. Manchester was full of Christmas shoppers, and here she was in the foyer of the Royal Exchange, standing in the jewellery booth, waiting for Anne Sargeant – poor Anne! – who was exchanging a pair of trousers and then would be having coffee with her. People brushed past Stella as they examined brooches, bracelets and scarves of exotic fabrics. The richness of it all added to Stella's euphoria. Next to her was a man with long dark hair tied into a pony-tail. She wanted to tap him on the shoulder and tell him what had happened to her. She and Heyside had won. She was going to have dinner with Jo McKenzie.

Next Thursday, and, sadly, not before, she could announce it to the Heyside members. They would be delighted. An evening in the Carlton International Hotel, and food too. Well, not too much, Stella hoped. The annual losses were due in at the end of December. She wondered what they would all look like dressed up. She felt quite maternal. Perhaps if she did buy the pendant, she could wear it with her cocktail dress on the night. Her dress was midnight blue, and tied around the middle was a wide black satin sash. She wondered how low the pendant would hang. Since the belt was high, the pendant might very well meet it, which would spoil the line. And then she remembered again. She had won. She would be meeting Jo.

'Stella!'

It was Anne. Her black trench coat was belted up tightly around her waist. She carried a parcel from an exclusive clothes shop in the Gardens.

'Let's get some coffee. I'm exhausted. Manchester's teeming this afternoon.'

They walked from the jewellery booth across the foyer of the theatre. It was even busy there. A long queue trailed from the box office, intent on buying tickets for the latest production, something light and entertaining for the Christmas season, no doubt. They went upstairs and joined the queue at the snack-bar. The idea of a cake to celebrate flashed across Stella's mind but was instantly dismissed. She decided she would be her slimmest ever for Jo. If she could lose about three pounds in the next fortnight, then she would be nearly eight and a half stone. She glanced at Anne. She was probably less. But Anne had not won the competition. The women moved past the salads, biscuits, cake, and ordered the coffee. They found a table by the window, overlooking the theatre foyer.

'Congratulations again, Stella. You must be delighted.'

'The group did do well. I'm pleased with them.'

'But you must have inspired them. Your results have always been good. It's your tremendous enthusiasm. I'm sure you deserve this, Stella.'

'To be honest, Anne, I was surprised that Liverpool were second. Whatever happened to your Upper Horton group? Last time I saw you, you said they were doing so well.'

Anne smiled ruefully.

'They were. It was Renie Cohen's daughter's wedding. Her only child. She'd actually arranged for the wedding itself to take place in the hotel, and the hotel suite was decorated to look like a castle in a fairy-tale. Renie was determined to make it the wedding of a lifetime. She had to be slim for it – well, at least for the pictures! And she'd invited the vast majority of the group – they all know each other in Upper Horton. They were all slimming for it.

'The wedding was last Sunday. Have you ever been to a Jewish wedding?'

'I am Jewish.'

'Really? I never would have guessed!'

Stella felt a momentary discomfort. But despite the

fact that Anne took a predominantly Jewish Slim-Plicity group, she had never betrayed any anti-Semitism.

'Well, then. I needn't tell you about the dinner. Renie told me they had ten courses. The meal alone lasted three hours. And apparently there were gâteaux later with the tea. Those women gorged themselves.'

Stella remembered scenes from her childhood; her mother at wedding parties, her aunts, in sleeveless se-quinned cocktail dresses, the loose flesh on the arms wobbling, young male cousins being sick in the Gents as the richness of the food rebelled with the alcohol, waitresses in black and white advancing with more and more dishes, menus embellished in silver and gold . . .

'Renie confessed that the next day she missed Rochelle so much, she ate to console herself. And anyway, she'd ruined her loss for that week so she thought she might as well eat what she wanted for the rest of the week. And so did the rest of the group. Last week fifteen members of Upper Horton ate *everything* they had deprived themselves of for the past eight weeks. That's why the group had a total gain last week.'

Anne laughed. Apparently she didn't care very much. Stella couldn't quite share her amusement, as it felt a little too familiar.

'You know what this means, Stella.'

'What?'

'You're bound to get Area Co-ordinator.'

'Not at all. It's got nothing to do with it.'

'It's bound to make an impression on the panel. It's as good as yours.'

'You know you've got just as good a chance as me.

Oh, I wish we weren't in competition like this!' said Stella, generously.

'I don't think we are,' said Anne.

Stella looked at Anne suspiciously. She did not trust her an inch. She knew something, and it was not clear exactly what it was she knew. But Stella did not really mind. She had won the competition. She would be meeting, speaking to, and having dinner with Jo McKenzie.

Sandra was by herself in the upstairs room at the Wellington. She took the opportunity to get a tissue out of her jeans pocket and blow her nose, loud and long. Her nose ached, and round the base it was sore and tender. Her head throbbed. Sandra was acutely miserable. She had a shocking cold. It seemed to have affected every part of her. Her face felt swollen, and her nose throbbed and pulsated with a life of its own. But that was not why she felt so depressed, she thought, as she slid her finger repeatedly along the edge of the table at which she was seated. Sometimes she enjoyed having a cold. The languor of it, the excuse it gave you for pampering yourself; these were positive. But she certainly didn't feel like packing when she got home after the FWSG meeting, as indeed she had to, for tomorrow she was due to return home for Christmas.

She would have liked to stay in Manchester a little longer, but her landlord wanted to do some repainting, and her last tutorial had been this morning. At home she would be able to look after herself. She sniffed. In a way, she was quite looking forward to Christmas. After the usual inquisition about the standard she was achieving in her essays, and her father's lamenting that an English degree would and could never lead to anything, she would go Christmas shopping in York with her mother and sister, cook things, have long evenings watching television in comparative luxury, sipping sherry and bringing out snacks from the kitchen. She could regress to the safety of just being a daughter. And then she could also look forward to seeing her old schoolfriends. Every vacation they all met up in town and went out for a pizza.

The nagging feeling returned. Something had disturbed her equilibrium, and the last stray thought was responsible. Her friends? She wondered if they would notice that she had lost weight. That was it. It was her weight again. She had been hoping that when she came home at Christmas her father, her friends, everyone would be knocked out by the new, slim Sandra. But she had lost less than a stone. It was something, but she knew how easy it would be to put it all back on just over the Christmas period. She could not imagine trying to deprive herself of food at this time of the year. She would have to go to have a pizza with her friends. And eat the Christmas dinner. All her efforts over the last term, sporadic as they had been, would be wasted. She was kidding herself if she ever thought there could be a long-term solution to the problem of weight. You ate, you enjoyed yourself, you put on weight, you felt guilty, you dieted, you got hungry, you ate, you enjoyed yourself – the cycle was endless. She was trapped by the inevitability of it. There seemed to be no escape. She was pinned to a wheel. Like the medieval Wheel of Fortune. Her mind strayed to her last essay on Chaucer.

The clock, with its roman figures, on the wall opposite her, announced that Liz, Martha, Emma and the others were late. Sandra had not waited downstairs for them because she did not want to buy herself a drink. Her father would be sure to inquire about the size of her overdraft. Another source of discontent. She felt in her other pocket for a Locket. She knew really that throat sweets had no curative properties whatsoever, but if you couldn't have them when you had a streaming cold, then when could you? She imagined she felt the antiseptic in the sweet attacking the germs in her throat. This came from her mother. Whenever she was ill as a child, her mother encouraged her to imagine her medicine as containing minute white soldiers, which killed all the germs in her body. Part of her still believed that medicine worked like that. The honey in the Locket slid down her throat. If only you could destroy the obsession with weight and food so easily.

She had hoped that joining the Fat Women's Support Group would have been her magic medicine. She really had tried to enjoy being fat. When she was with Liz, Martha, and especially Emma, it did not seem to matter that she was overweight. And yet, alone, lying in bed and feeling her stomach, she knew it did matter to her, and it mattered a lot. She wanted to be slim. But she also wanted to eat.

She had been to Slim-Plicity that night. She had in fact lost one and a half pounds, half a pound more than Helen. The thought of Helen filled her with delight. The best thing about this term had been Helen. Sandra liked herself for being able to make such a good friend, and particularly for having the courage to step outside her own social circle. Perhaps she was growing up. But also she had been able to help Helen. Her idea about the 'New Opportunities for Women' course had taken root. Helen had spoken about it with enthusiasm tonight. She did not stay for the whole meeting, as she too had a cold, and they had said their goodbyes there. The children had sent Sandra a Christmas card and had drawn a picture on it. It was in her pocket with her tissues and throat sweets. She would see Helen again as soon as she got back in January.

Both of them had told Stella that they were leaving. She had said it was a great shame. She'd said they were two of her best losers, and that if they changed their mind she would be delighted to have them back. She'd said it was all the more a pity because Heyside had won the autumn promotion, and that on the fourteenth of December the whole group was to attend a celebration buffet at the Carlton International Hotel and of course she and Helen were invited. Helen had said that it wasn't really for her, that sort of occasion, and Sandra had explained that she would be home in Selby. Nevertheless Stella had pressed upon her an invitation card to the buffet in the Kitchener Suite at 7.30 p.m.

Thinking about it now, it all seemed ridiculous to Sandra. Fancy having a celebration buffet – eating! – to celebrate a weight loss. The whole group ought to go circuit training. She smiled at the thought. She thought of the group flaunting its success at the Carlton International Hotel, all dressed up to the nines. Probably the press would be there, and report the occasion fully. And after Christmas thousands more

Mancunian women would be tempted to join the tread-mill of dieting, food deprivation, bingeing, guilt ... Sandra felt angry. But she needed to blow her nose again.

She wondered if there was a bin in the room in which she could deposit the sodden tissue. Just then the door opened and Liz strode in, followed by Emma and Martha.

'So you're here, Sandra! We were waiting for you downstairs. No one else seems to have turned up.'

'I thought I'd come straight up. I didn't feel like a drink.'

'We may as well get started.'

The three women drew out seats from the table and joined Sandra. There was an uncomfortable silence. Liz broke it.

'I expect it's the weather. I thought Debbie would be here.'

'Can we have a meeting with just four of us?' inquired Emma.

'Certainly,' answered Martha. 'There is no formal structure in the group, and so there can be no quorum.' She undid the toggles on her red duffle-coat as if to confirm her intention to stay. Sandra found them strangely pathetic, abandoned as they seemed to be by the other members. It was nearly a month since the picket. No new members had appeared as a result, and the local radio item on their activities was all the pub-licity they received. There had been two heavily theoretical meetings since the picket, and Sandra sensed morale was low. Or rather, she thought it ought to be. But Liz was eternally cheerful.

'Right, sisters. I think we need to do something to get us out of the doldrums. We've all been suffering from anticlimax since our picket, successful as it was. I think perhaps the time has come to organize a national conference of fat women. There are bound to be groups in other parts of the country; I know there's one in London.'

'That's not a bad idea, Liz,' said Martha. 'But it isn't enough. We're not going to change attitudes by talk alone. We've got to fight. If necessary, we've got to meet brutality with resistance. I'm in favour of more direct action. I'm prepared to get arrested if needs be.'

'That's ridiculous, Martha. It won't solve anything. Look, Liz, Martha.' Emma breathed deeply. 'Like you, I think that society gives fat women a raw deal. It's true; we are mocked, we are figures of fun, and this ridicule affects all women who are overweight. And I agree that it's the result of a male-dominated society. But I don't think that a public fight is the answer. I admire you both for your stand at Du Mont. But I was terrified and insulted. It just wasn't for me.'

Martha glared at her. Sandra was rapt with attention.

'Surely body weight is a personal issue. Every woman should be able to decide what weight she wants to be. Not everyone wants to be fat. For some women it might be right to lose weight. But what women ought to be doing is to work together to discover what the answer is for them as individuals. You can't change attitudes that have hardened over centuries just by a picket here or there. But you can change your personal attitude. Can't we just support each other?'

'That's giving in, Emma. It's as much as to say we're prepared to put up with the oppression of fat women.' Liz's tone was insistent.

'No, Liz. If there are any effective ways in which we can make life easier for fat women, then we should. But I don't see why at the same time, we can't investigate why we as individuals have become overweight. Some sort of therapy or analysis could be a great source of strength.'

'Overweight! You said "overweight", and that wasn't the first time. I thought we'd agreed that the word was innately critical of fat women,' said Martha, smugly.

Sandra listened to them squabble. She couldn't decide who to agree with, with whom to cast her lot. What Emma said interested her immensely. She herself would love the opportunity to work through her own attitudes towards weight. But it did seem rather self-regarding, when there were so many other less privileged fat women without the money or ability to have or profit from therapeutic analysis. She fumbled in her pocket and discovered to her horror she had run out of clean tissues. She sniffed loudly, and her ears rang, distancing the sound of argument from her. Her head throbbed. But she no longer felt sorry for herself. She watched her three friends and pitied them. They could not agree; their support had diminished; their initial enthusiasm had dissolved into acrimony. And she had just left Slim-Plicity, where the glamorous, competent Stella had informed her that Heyside had won the competition, and were off to the Carlton International Hotel. Slim-Plicity had everything. There were easily over fifty women there most Thursdays, and each of them experienced the pleasure of losing weight, all of them a constant reproach to fat women everywhere. The contrast between the excited hubbub of the Slim-Plicity meeting she had just left, and the bitter despondency she was seeing now, struck her forcibly. It wasn't fair. Her friends were the underdogs. It just wasn't fair.

'I know what we can do!' interrupted Sandra. 'Slim-Plicity's buffet.'

The women looked at her quizzically. Sandra realized with horror that she had never informed them that she was a card-carrying member of Slim-Plicity. She would have to devise a cover for herself.

'You see, I have a friend. A friend of mine – Helen, Helen Greenwood – *she* goes to a slimming club, Slim-Plicity. Actually it meets across the road from here in the Legion. On a Thursday night too. She told me that the group had lost so much weight that it was having a celebration buffet at the Carlton International Hotel soon, I think on the fourteenth, but I can check that. The press is sure to be there, photographers too, I daresay. It's a blatant revelling in the cult of slimness. *That's* where we should be – in the Carlton – demonstrating against Slim-Plicity!'

Martha smiled at her.

'An excellent idea. We'll do it!'

'Excellent!' echoed Liz. 'Let's demonstrate against slimming clubs. An absolutely appropriate target. Well done, Sandra.'

Their praise was like a narcotic to her. Sandra babbled on.

'Yes, precisely. They offer women short-term weight losses, but foster an obsession with slimming that the women never lose. They hook you in. They tell you that you can't lose weight without them and rob you of any sense of control you have over your own eating. Because the organizers of these clubs, they're only in it for the money. It costs nearly three pounds a week. And the diet is extremely difficult to follow. It's based on a system of traffic lights . . .'

'You seem to know a lot about it, Sandra.'

'Yes. Well, Helen tells me.'

'But you're absolutely right. These clubs are iniquitous,' said Liz. 'We'll do it. We'll picket their celebration buffet. Get us as much information as you can, Sandra.'

'I can tell you now. I must, as I can't be there myself. I'm going home for Christmas tomorrow.' She sneezed. 'Has anyone got a tissue?'

As they walked down the stairs together, Emma whispered to Sandra, 'I know what would be good for that cold. Southern Comfort.'

'I can't . . .'

'It's my treat. I work and you don't. Can you stay and have a drink?'

Sandra relented. The Wellington was busy, and they had to share a table with a couple who ignored them, being very wrapped up in one another. The heat of the whisky liqueur relaxed Sandra almost immediately. Her cold symptoms seemed to recede.

'Your friend Helen who goes to Slim-Plicity. Was that the same Helen we had a drink with a few weeks ago?'

'Yes. That's her.'

'I liked her, Sandra. Is she going to the buffet?'

'No. It doesn't really appeal to her. What do you think of the idea of picketing it, Emma? You didn't say anything at the meeting.'

Sandra knew she was on dangerous ground. She found it hard to cope with criticism of her ideas, and she particularly valued Emma. She tensed as she waited for Emma's reply.

'You're right in your criticisms of Slim-Plicity. I thought you put it very well. But I still don't think it will achieve much. Think how pathetic we'll look compared to all the Slim-Plicity members dressed to kill.'

All Sandra's self-respect drained away. She had been a fool. Carried away on a wave of pity, she'd made an absolutely ludicrous suggestion. She'd betrayed Stella and everyone else. And she had nothing against them as individuals. She was a traitor. Once again her besetting sin – the desire to win approval from those around her – had led her into a mess. And it was too late to do anything about it. She didn't even have the energy to lift up her glass of Southern Comfort to her lips. She hated and despised herself bitterly. She said nothing to Emma in reply.

'What's wrong, Sandra?'

A tear rolled down Sandra's face.

'Oh, God, I'm so useless.'

Emma handed her another tissue. Sandra blew her nose again, and felt it become more swollen. She could no longer breathe through it, and took gulps of air through her mouth.

'I shouldn't have mentioned the bloody buffet. I've

just gone and put my foot in it again. When will I grow up?'

'Don't be so hard on yourself. You never know what may come out of it. Poor old Sandra. I noticed you looked miserable this evening. Is it just the cold, or is there anything else?'

Sandra was flooded with an overwhelming desire to tell Emma everything. She derived a great deal of comfort and security from conversations with older women – she always had done – and now, awash with self-pity, the temptation to wallow in her own problems was irresistible. She knew she was being self-obsessed, but this time she would give in to it.

'It's no use. I don't want to be fat, but I don't want to diet. I keep thinking about food and weight all the time. And I hate myself for it.'

'But nobody else hates you, Sandra.'

'That doesn't matter. You must know what it's like – that awful feeling of shame. I see people looking at me and thinking what a pig I am, thinking that I have no self-control.'

'It's all in your own mind.'

'This extra weight isn't.'

'No, but you can decide how to look at it. You don't have to be angry with yourself, or angry with society. Accept the weight is there: then decide what to do about it.'

'But I don't get it. Why did you join the Fat Women's Support Group at all?'

Emma laughed.

'Well, I must admit that at the time I also felt full of anger. But a lot's happened to me recently, both in my personal life, and also professionally. At work I was sent on an assertiveness course, and through that I met a therapist, who I've seen once or twice, and it's made quite a difference to me. She's an American, Gill Goldstein.'

'How can therapy help?'

'You look at your past history – your relationship with your mother – that sort of thing. And you begin to realize that maybe you're not to blame.'

'But it *can't* be my mother's fault. She's wonderful. She's supported me and my sister through everything, and even now I can speak freely to her. I had a lovely childhood.'

Sandra sounded quite dismayed. For a transitory moment she would have loved to have an evil mother. But alas, it was not to be. Sandra continued.

'And *she*'s not fat. She's the Jane Fonda type, and I'm sure I've disappointed her being this size, even though she would never say. She's a town councillor this year.'

'Your mother sounds a lot to live up to.'

Sandra was silent. Emma smiled.

Sandra began hesitantly, 'So it might be my mother?'

'Careful! I didn't say it was your mother's fault either. And anyway, I can't think of a more horrific prospect for women than to have the ills of the world cast on their shoulders because they weren't perfect mothers.'

'But my mother was perfect.'

'Perhaps that's your problem.'

The two women laughed. Sandra's cold was beginning to feel better.

'No, what I mean is that your weight obsession is not your mother's fault, but an understanding of the nature of childhood can sometimes help you to accept yourself. And there's more to it than that. Very often the weight obsession is a way of avoiding worrying about something else more important. Overeating followed by remorse can block out the real problem.'

'What do you mean?'

'Take my example. I put on over two stone in the last year of my marriage. I couldn't face up to the fact I'd married the wrong man. So I ate to punish myself and to punish him. At least it seems like that now. Len, who I'm living with, likes me big. I've become relaxed about the whole issue. I've stopped bingeing, and I think I may have even lost some. Don't misunderstand me – I'm not saying a man is the answer. But when the real problem is tackled, the weight obsession can recede.'

'But I don't have any problems, apart from the usual ones like money and essay deadlines.'

'Why is it that sometimes when I hear you talk, Sandra, you sound as if you hate yourself so much?'

'I'm fat.'

'Any other reason?'

'I'm indecisive, I take everybody's side, I can't make up my own mind, my father thinks I'm wasting my time doing an English degree, I've no strength of character – that sort of thing.'

'Gill Goldstein would say that weaknesses are often strengths. So perhaps you have the gift of seeing things from everybody's point of view, and to listen carefully to both sides of an argument. And that you have a delightful humility.'

Sandra said nothing. She could not dispute the logic; for her it could not be an emotional reality.

'And your father thinks you're wasting your time studying English. Why are you studying English?'

'I love it.'

'Do you know what you want to be?'

'I haven't got a clue. Lots of things appeal to me.'

'What do you enjoy doing apart from English?'

'I like people. The best thing this term has been Helen – oh, and you! I mean, getting to know someone out of my own social circle, and really liking her, and I think I've helped her too. She's going to do a "New Opportunities for Women" course!'

'There. You can feel pleased with yourself about that. Have you ever thought about teaching on a course like that yourself?'

'No.'

'Why not? I cán't think of anything more fulfilling than helping women who've missed out in some way, and you'd still be in touch with your own subject.'

Sandra's face shone.

'You mean I could be an English teacher?'

'It's a possibility.'

Suddenly Sandra saw herself holding a pile of books, and walking into a room full of women – and Helen would be there – ready to teach, to share what she had been learning. She turned radiant to Emma.

'And I wouldn't need to feel guilty any more about getting so much selfish pleasure out of reading. I could share it all! Why hadn't I thought of this? I suppose I've spent too long worrying about my weight! Perhaps I ought to train to teach children too. I like children.'

'You needn't decide on everything now. You've got plenty of time. But it sounds like a good idea. I'm quite jealous of you. I'd love someone as enthusiastic as you teaching me.'

Sandra bent over and kissed her.

'Oh damn, I bet I've given you my cold. But I feel so much better. Getting sudden revelations like this, it just doesn't seem real. I can't believe it. Can I?'

CHAPTER FOURTEEN

Emma idly wondered why there should be a war memorial inside the lobby of the Carlton International Hotel. In fact she stood below a large black statue of a uniformed soldier, apparently ready to charge into battle. As her friends were, she thought. On the wall opposite was a list of the staff who had served in both wars. It all seemed incongruous set against the plush red carpet, the marble pillars, and the glimpse of the splendid interior that Emma received as visitors pushed past her to enter. She knew she was early, but it had been convenient for Len to drop her off at this time. Most of the people going into the hotel seemed to be Christmas revellers, out on office parties. One was apparently a fancy-dress party. Unless, that is, she was hallucinating when a Red Indian chief in full regalia marched up the stairs and into the hotel. Emma was feeling increasingly conspicuous, particularly as she was dressed quite plainly in a large fawn trench coat. She thought she might be more comfortable inside, and so pushed open the centre set of double doors, and crossed the threshold.

It was magnificent. No, it wasn't: it was gross. In front of her was a massive chandelier dripping cut glass, forming a huge centre-piece in the reception area. The staircase that swept up in front of her was carpeted in dark red, and reminded her of a B movie screen set. To her left was a long panelled reception area, where smartly uniformed girls were speaking on telephones, and getting keys from pigeon-holes. She noticed that also to her left was a board announcing the events that night, and she moved towards it to scrutinize it more carefully. Yes. In the middle it read SLIM-PLICITY. KITCHENER SUITE. She felt herself nudged by another woman.

After a fraction of a second her new companion asked, 'Do you know where the Kitchener Suite is, love?'

Emma turned to see a large middle-aged lady, still in her coat, carrying both a large black handbag and a canvas shopping bag. Her hair, however, was beautifully permed.

'Sorry, I don't. Are you with Slim-Plicity?'

'Yes, ducks. I'm here for the buffet. And I'm absolutely starving.'

'Perhaps if you ask one of the receptionists, they'll help you.'

Emma noticed that as this woman went over to the reception desk she popped a boiled sweet into her mouth from her coat pocket. She herself wondered where the Kitchener Suite might be, and looked upwards to check for directions. Sure enough a sign pointed off to the right, so Emma moved on in that direction. The entrance to the suite was on her left, and the door stood ajar, revealing a medium-sized hall, lined on three of its sides with tables containing food. The carpets and festooned drapes were all in pale green and lemon yellow. As yet the room seemed empty. Two or three smartly dressed women stood at one side deep in conversation. She heard footsteps behind her, and turned to see the woman she had spoken to previously. To avoid further conversation she walked hastily on. Reaching the bar, she turned, and retraced her steps to the reception area to wait for Liz and Martha. Yet again she was struck with the sheer impossibility of their task. The weight, the grandeur of the hotel oppressed her; their picket would have no impact; yet again they would be ridiculed. It was then that Emma knew she had to talk them out of it. Hopefully only Liz and Martha would turn up; perhaps with luck she could convert the evening to just a night out in Manchester. She swallowed and breathed deeply.

Stella's mouth was dry, and she took several deep breaths as Linda had instructed her, in order to allay her nervousness. It didn't work. Her hands, her legs, felt as shaky as they did before. She tried laughing at herself, as indeed she might. This was the evening she had dreamed of for years. She was actually going to meet Jo McKenzie. And indeed she was ecstatically, wildly happy. But terrified too. She remembered being in a similar state on her wedding day. Driving to the registry office on that Saturday morning she had clutched her bouquet of flowers higher and higher until they masked her face as each muscle contracted with tension. And now even her relaxation exercises were not enough to calm her.

She checked her appearance yet again in the full-length mirror in the Ladies. One bonus of her physical reactions to stress was that her stomach muscles contracted too; she had spent most of the day in her bathroom at home; her stomach was empty, and, as she pulled it in, she could see from her sideways reflection that it was almost concave. Wonderful. And her cocktail dress was quite splendid. She peered closely at her face. Her make-up was immaculate. Gingerly, she smiled at herself. She smiled more widely, imagining she was speaking to Jo; she smiled again, with suppressed laughter, as she realized how ridiculous she must look to anyone coming in just now. She checked her watch. Seven twenty. Not too early for her to arrive, and taking her small clutch bag, she left the room through two sets of heavy doors, and made her way to the Kitchener Suite.

It was as yet quite empty. In one corner she saw Deborah, and her personal assistant from HQ. With her she recognized the Area Co-ordinator from the north-east, who was hoping to run a similar event in the new year. The fourth woman she also recognized. Jo was not there. Perhaps she was still in her room. With a lurch of her stomach, she considered the possibility that Jo would not be there. Perhaps her flight was delayed, or she was unavoidably detained in the States. Stella was too terrified even to ask if this might be the case. But the four women smiled at her, and beckoned for her to join them. Perhaps it would be all right. As she moved across the room she glimpsed Maureen, already arrived, standing suspiciously closely to the open sandwiches, eyeing them with a lasciviousness which Stella found somewhat embarrassing. She joined her colleagues.

'You look wonderful, Stella.'

'Thank you. What a gorgeous dress, Deborah. I don't think I've seen it before.'

No, Stella could not bring herself to mention Jo. But Deborah had not said anything to suggest that things had gone wrong. She tried to relax, and forced herself to watch her Heyside members arrive and look around them. They seemed impressed with what they found. Their pleasure reassured Stella, and she decided to join them. Piped music suddenly filled the room.

Maureen positioned herself close to one corner and surveyed the food. She was satisfied. There was plenty of it. However, most of it seemed bite-sized. This dismayed her slightly, but then, she could always have more! She had put her handbag and canvas bag out of harm's way under the table. Unhampered, she regarded the food with fresh attention. Near her was a plate piled high with slivers of toast, decorated with smoked salmon and half an olive. Maureen thought they could have been a bit more generous with the salmon. The contents of the next plate she could not identify at all. It looked like balls of puff pastry, un-adorned. How strange! Why eat pastry if there was nothing inside. She glimpsed in addition egg mayonnaise open sandwiches, small dishes of nuts, crisps – again, very few of those – and what looked like a cottage cheese dip, surrounded by strips of raw vegetables. Fancy going to a buffet to eat slices of carrot! In the distance, along the table, Maureen could see a bowl of fresh fruit, and thought that behind that there *might* be a gâteau, but it was impossible to see.

How very different from Maureen's fiftieth, which took place last Friday at the Wellington. In the end she did not buy a dress, but on Angie's advice purchased a grey voile skirt, with a flowery silk blouse. And she had looked smashing. Lucky there was a bit of room in the waistband, and the food was spectacular. They'd ordered cold chicken, and it came with all sorts of trimmings and salads, but these salads were dripping with dressings. And for dessert three different kinds of gâteaux, and cheesecake, and Maureen had had the lot. After all, she was the birthday girl. She had got gloriously drunk too. She blushed to remember the rest. What a do!

And the next day the family had all come round and told her she had to leave Slim-Plicity. They had said they were fed up with it. And she'd agreed. She only asked that she should be able to attend this buffet. It would be her chance to eat everything they had forbidden her. But in fact the food seemed rather paltry. But she would do her best. She wondered again what was in those puff pastry balls.

'Maureen! What a lovely skirt and blouse! Are they new?'

'Yes, Stella. I bought them for my fiftieth. The skirt's a bit tight round the waist, though.'

'Well, we can soon see to that.'

That's what you think, thought Maureen. Stella moved on to greet some of the other newly arrived slimmers, and Maureen realized that while she had been contemplating the food, a waiter in a maroon waistcoat had begun to serve glasses of wine. She hurried across the room to get some. In the queue, she listened to her fellow members.

'I've left all my calorie allowance for this evening. What about you?'

'I've starved myself today. I've got all my Ambers to have as well.'

'I don't think you're supposed to do that. I think Stella said so once.'

'Florence over there, she's had all her allowances today.'

Maureen praised God that she had done with all of that, for now. She was going to eat with unashamed pleasure. No more reds, ambers and greens for her. Certainly no more greens! No more cabbage! No more cauliflower! The wine was rather dry but was having the desired effect. And it sharpened Maureen's appetite.

She was puzzled to see that no one had started eating yet. She wasn't too sure what the rules were in these formal situations. At her parties, people started eating immediately. But perhaps everyone here was waiting for a signal. Or were they all too embarrassed to begin? She moved back to the buffet tables on her self-imposed sentry duty. What was in those puff pastry balls? She watched the Slim-Plicity officials gather together at the front of the hall. Watching them, her hand, an independent agent, sought the puff pastry balls and secreted one. She popped one in her mouth. Pâté!

'Good evening, ladies. I cannot tell you how much pleasure it gives me to see you all here tonight, looking so glamorous. Even those of you with a bit to go look ravishing. I'm sure none of you regret having . . .'

One more. Liver pâté, probably.

'. . . effort you have put into this. I know what an

inspiration Stella has been for you, always encouraging you to . . .'

Two together; they were very small.

'. . . a token of our esteem for your efforts, and I would ask Stella to come and receive this certificate to commemorate . . .'

The smoked salmon bites. Just a couple of those. Don't care what anyone thinks.

'I think you're wonderful, all of you. Thank you, Heyside, for having worked so hard so that I can share this moment of triumph with you . . .'

Triumph. That was it. Maureen felt triumphant. And since no one else would have the courage to eat tonight, there would be all the more for her. She snatched another pâté ball.

'Thank you, Stella. As you know, ladies, Stella will not be with you for the rest of the evening, as she has been chosen to have dinner with Jo McKenzie, our founder member, who has flown in from the States. And I now invite the rest of you to join in a toast . . .'

Toast. More smoked salmon. Just a small egg sandwich. Mmm. Lovely.

'The food is here for your enjoyment, and I am sure that Stella has shown you how to enjoy food without taking it to excess. Well done, Heyside!'

Maureen realized that a lady behind her had taken a side plate, serviette and a fork, and clearly you were expected to fill a plate with the goodies on offer rather than just pick. Well, that was all right by her. She also took a plate, and with gay abandon piled it as high as she could. Luckily she had finished her wine, so she had two hands free. She ate with relish, and glanced at the table. Yes. She had guessed correctly. Everyone was outdoing each other in not eating. Most of the members were gathered around the cottage cheese dip. She would have a second plateful before starting on the dessert.

Yes. There was one fruit gâteau. She took a slice, and a bit of the next one that had fallen on to the plate. Nearby was a jug of cream. She poured over a generous helping. Delicious. She looked down the table again. Her waistband was cutting into her flesh. She didn't think even she could manage any more – yet. But what if an over-efficient member of staff decided to clear the plates away? Maureen, however, had come prepared.

She returned to her original position along the table, bent down, and retrieved her canvas shopping bag. Furtively she scooped up the remaining pâté balls and put them into a brown paper bag. She found a white paper bag, which she used for the smoked salmon bites. She turned to discover three fascinated Slim-Plicity members watching her.

'Just removing these out of temptation's way, my dears.'

Emma brought back three pints of bitter to the table she had found in the bar of the Carlton International Hotel. The fates had been on her side. Liz and Martha had been late, detained by unusually heavy traffic. Thus they had missed the Slim-Plicity members coming into the buffet, and Emma had initially suggested that they wait until the end. So she had brought them into the bar. The only table that they could find free was along one side of the room close to the entrance to the restaurant. Used to unpretentious local pubs, the women spent some time orientating themselves in these new, grandiose surroundings. The bar was large, high-ceilinged, and dark red festooned curtains drooped unevenly down the windows. In the centre of the room played a small artificial fountain, illuminated by hidden fairy lights. Despite the space, the atmosphere was oppressive. Cigar smoke hung in the air; the loud, intrusive, flashy playing of a piano prevented any intimate conversation. Men – surely they were all businessmen – wore suits, slopped their beer, and laughed loudly. There were hardly any women in the bar at all.

'What a dreadful place,' said Martha.

'I wonder what it would be like to eat here?' inquired Liz, gazing towards the entrance of the restaurant.

The restaurant lobby, accessible through a curtained arch, was only a few feet in front of them. It was certainly the sort of restaurant where one would expect to eat rare steak, and rich foreign food, according to the expectations aroused by the décor. Like the bar, there were dark red drapes everywhere. Opposite the mahogany reception desk was a heavy glass cabinet, and below it a small table, draped in red. A menu card stood on it. Liz would have gone over to investigate further but a man had come to block the way.

'Do you know how long the buffet is scheduled to last?'

'No,' said Emma. 'It's been running for about forty minutes now. I'd guess perhaps another half an hour.'

'Have you seen my placard, Emma?'

Liz vanished below the table, and awkwardly re-emerged with a large placard that she turned towards Emma. On it was a cartoon of a tall, fat woman, with a red coat held together by a white rope round the waist. She wore what looked like a red nightcap, and high boots. It read MOTHER CHRISTMAS SAYS SHE'S PROUD TO BE FAT!

'No,' said Emma. 'You can't use that.'

'I know it's not as overtly political as our usual material, but I thought it was seasonal.' Liz was hurt.

'Look. I'm going to come clean with you both. I'm against this. I don't want to take part in it. There are only three of us — two of you — and a hotel full of drunken business men.'

'But we're not interested in them,' countered Martha. 'We are demonstrating against Slim-Plicity and bring a message of hope to the misguided women who are trying to lose weight.'

'I agree with Martha,' said Liz solidly.

'But do you think that those women will be ready to listen to us after being fêted and congratulated by the organization? I can't imagine a less receptive audience.'

'All the more credit to us for trying,' Martha spoke this slowly. A heavy depression descended upon Emma. Nothing would stop these women. Already they had attracted some quizzical looks. Emma felt powerless. Perhaps, she thought wildly, there would be a fire alert, a bomb scare, anything to prevent her friends from making a laughing-stock of themselves. But Liz and Martha continued to drink their beer and checked their watches.

*

'It's ten to eight now, Stella. You'd better pop over to the restaurant to meet Jo.'

Stella's heart beat increased. It was really going to happen. Strange how she had imagined this moment so many times, always in a different situation, never quite like this. But here she was, in her new midnight blue cocktail dress, about to meet Jo McKenzie. She felt schoolgirlish, inadequate.

'Where do I . . .?'

'We arranged for you to meet in the restaurant lobby. Turn right outside the suite and it's just through the bar.'

Stella nodded, her mouth dry. She slipped out of the room.

'Look, Liz.' Emma felt that sometimes Liz could be more reasonable. 'We can abandon this, just go for a drink elsewhere, and then plan that national conference you were talking of. And we could write to major clothing manufacturers to ask them about their policy regarding fat women. Anything, so long as you drop this.'

'Sorry, Emma. We're here now. My instinct tells me it's right to go ahead.'

'Finish your beer, Liz. I suggest we set up in about five minutes. Some women are sure to be leaving early.'

Emma was angry and distressed. The silence between them was almost palpable. Together, abstracted, they watched a slim, attractive young woman pass in front of them towards the restaurant. Emma imagined she must be meeting someone. She fleetingly thought how uncomfortable that stiff, ruched cocktail dress must be.

Stella stepped up the three steps leading to the restaurant. She looked briefly around her. She could see no sign of Jo McKenzie. But of course. It was quite proper that she should be here to wait for Jo. She clutched her handbag more tightly.

Her equilibrium was slightly disturbed by the man standing next to her. He was in his forties, and thoroughly repulsive. He had taken off the jacket of his suit, and stood there in a shirt, open at the collar. The shirt was too tight for his bursting stomach and the buttons pulled. Through the spaces between the buttons sprouted masses of black curly hair. Revolting, thought Stella. He was balding too. It wasn't his popping eyes, that seemed to leer at her, that disgusted her. Nor his heavy jowls, and the beads of sweat that formed on his glistening forehead. (He had been drinking, evidently.) No. It was his sheer bulk. The man was fat. Her mother always called a man's stomach a 'corporation', meaning to be euphemistic, and so Stella had always imagined these fat men to be heads of corporations, and therefore very rich. This man certainly looked rich too. His gold watch was massive. He wore several rings. His corporation (Stella used the word in her mind) hung out over the top of his trousers. She shuddered. For a moment she imagined he was smiling at her, smiling lasciviously. She wished Jo would hurry up. She looked away. The man stepped closer. How dare he spoil this precious moment!

'Stella Martin?' He spoke in a mid-American drawl.

She glared at him, not comprehending why he should know her name.

'I'm Joe McKenzie.'

Emma watched that fat, oily man standing in the restaurant lobby approach the girl in the cocktail dress. Surely she can't be meeting him. Emma stared as he approached her; they spoke briefly. Never had she seen a woman look more shocked; never a man more amused. The woman walked away sharply, crossed in front of Emma, leaned against the wall, and for a moment Emma thought she was going to faint. Emma rose quickly and approached her.

'What's wrong? Can I help?'

'I'm not well. I want to get out of here.'

'Do you have a coat?'

Emma gesticulated to her friends, but there was no need. They too had witnessed the unusual scene, and Liz, sensing the need for immediate action, was ready to help. Within minutes, Stella was whisked out of the hotel, supported by Emma and Liz. Martha brought up the rear, trailing the placards and banners.

The slap of the cold night air shocked Stella. Nothing was real any more; there was no more sanity, nothing to live for. It did not matter to her that she was being led by these three strange women, conscious as she was of their good intentions. Just now, she was incapable of thought.

Soon they reached Piccadilly Gardens. The darkness was periodically illuminated by the flashing of Christmas lights; wind gusted on the pathway blowing up scraps of paper that swirled around Stella's legs. She was guided to an empty bench facing a square grassy area. She realized she had never been in Piccadilly Gardens before. It was odd, really, when you thought about it, how little one knew of the places one lived in. She stared into the darkness.

'Do you want to tell us what happened?'

Stella frowned as if she were trying to remember. Emma was concerned.

'Sometimes it helps, talking about it.'

'There isn't such a person as Jo McKenzie. It was that man. They tricked me. It's all a trick. A cheat.'

Her voice trailed away.

'Explain to us. Please.'

With a huge effort of will, Stella began again. She spoke without emotion.

'I'm the Heyside Slim-Plicity group leader. My group were having a buffet to celebrate their weight loss. I was to meet Jo McKenzie, our – their – American founder member. I used to worship her. But she doesn't exist. There's just a man, that man you saw. He laughed at me. "Jo McKenzie" was just a publicity device, a front. A team of PR men had invented her, he told me. And I fell for it. I fell for the image. He told me that Anne and Deborah thought it would be funny, when I realized she – I mean he – was a man. But it's shattered everything.'

'I'm not surprised,' said Martha. 'Slim-Plicity is run for a profit. It's a business organization. And men get fat while women starve.' She evinced a grim satisfaction. Emma kicked her sharply in the shin.

'But, you see, I can't go on. I can't go back to Slim-Plicity. It was my job.'

The women were silent. Stella began to wonder what

252

it would be like without Slim-Plicity. She would have to find other work. She would have to tell Richard, her mother. She pictured the puzzlement of her Heyside members when they discovered she wasn't coming back. She in turn was betraying them. At that thought tears began to form.

'Oh, God!'

She sobbed bitterly. Emma hugged her, and without thinking Stella gave herself to the embrace. Wordlessly she accepted Emma's support. There were moments of blackness. As her heaving sobs died down, Stella became conscious once more of her surroundings. Who was this woman hugging her closely? Her mother? The large, soft body was familiar and soothing. No, a stranger. Stella tensed again, pulled away.

'I'm sorry. I'm ever so sorry. I'm all right now.'

'No, you're not,' said Liz with decision. 'And we're not leaving you until you are. If you like we'll drive you home. We've got a Transit near by.'

Stella looked at her rescuers in turn, as they bent eagerly towards her. All of them were fat. In her wonder she spoke.

'It's funny really. I've spent years trying to help fat women get thin, and now I'm thin and you're helping me – no, not to get fat . . .'

She was confused.

'I don't want to diet,' Liz asserted. 'I'm quite happy being fat. We all are. There is a world outside Slim-Plicity. We believe that it's chiefly men that have propagated the image of the slim woman as ideal. Dieting is a form of subordination to men. Look. Look at Slim-Plicity. Run by a man – for his profit and delight.'

Stella remembered the way he leered at her. She nodded. Liz, encouraged, went on.

'You mustn't feel bad about having made a mistake. It's easy to do. We'd come tonight to demonstrate against Slim-Plicity.'

'How did you know?'

'Sandra Coverdale, another one of us said . . .'

'Sandra Coverdale? She belongs to Slim-Plicity!'

Emma looked at Liz and Stella; she thought of Sandra.

'So you've both been helping her! Sandra must have belonged to both of us.'

Liz was not listening.

'I know you must feel as if everything you've worked for has ended, but you must try to see it as ultimately a good thing. You don't have to diet. Remember that. Food is a life-force, and we all need it.'

Stella drank down this new orthodoxy in gulps. Men were to blame. (Well, not Richard, perhaps.) And you don't have to diet. Food is life. Food. Suddenly she was aware of how very hungry she felt. She had not eaten all day. Perhaps her weakness was due to that . . .

'Were you going to eat in the hotel? You must be hungry now,' Emma suggested.

Stella smiled at her with a child's delight.

'I know!' cried Liz. 'Let's all go out and eat. Let's celebrate food and life and women!'

CHAPTER FIFTEEN

'Probably he suffered more than she did.'

The class exploded into outraged laughter. Typical! You could tell a man had written it. The tutor tried to calm them down. Helen was thoroughly enjoying herself. She knew really what Lawrence was trying to say: that Will Brangwen's emotional sufferings were more acute than Anna Brangwen's labour pains, but she had to admit that Lawrence did for that moment sound so very male-centred. It was ridiculous. And she had to join in the female camaraderie that D. H. Lawrence always engendered. How could a man say these things about women! The class was brought together. It was hard for Helen to decide what she enjoyed more: the intellectual discoveries she had made on this 'New Opportunities for Women' course, or the heady feeling of belonging to a group of women all in the same position as her.

The classroom in the Adult Education Centre looked out on to a dirty courtyard where scraps of last autumn's withered leaves still clogged up gutters. But the bright, fine, spring sunlight illuminated the scene. Helen answered it with a rising sense of exhilaration. For the last eight Tuesday mornings she had dropped Katy off at play group and had come straight here for the start of the 'New Opportunities' class. It was actually a day school. In the morning she studied literature; nineteenth and twentieth-century novels. Before lunch there were counselling, study skills and self-esteem sessions; and in the afternoon, after a pub lunch, the industrial revolution in the north-west. The idea was to show the women how much they were able to do. And Helen had been delighted by her own capacity for understanding. True, her first essay was an ordeal, but Sandra's advice had been invaluable.

So was the tumble-drier. Helen had pointed out to Tony that if the business was doing well, they could at last afford one. He was a bit taken aback; Tony was a traditionalist, and thought also, that washing smelt better hanging on a line. Helen had suggested then in that case he might like to hang the washing out. They bought a tumble-drier.

However, Tony was pleased about her embarking on this course. In fact, he had got into the habit of taking the kids out on a Sunday afternoon so she could get on with her notes, reading, essays, or whatever. She was currently researching for an essay on Lawrence and women. And here she was in class, not really concentrating on the discussion! She was invaded with a feeling of well-being, and leaned back in her chair. Of course, there was the ironing to do when she got home, and she hadn't yet decided what they were all going to have for dinner that night. But at least the housework wasn't *everything*!

One comforting thing to come out of the study skills session last week was that all the women on the course had the same problems as she did; no sooner did Helen sit down to concentrate when either a child interrupted, or more often, she herself began to wonder, did they have enough bread, how would she fit in the visit to her mother? It was as if she'd lost the power to concentrate. But all her friends on the course found this too. Their tutor had pointed out to them that they should see this ability to think of several different things at once as a strength, rather than simply as the inability to concentrate. It was something, she said, that men could not do, and that women could. It was true! How often Tony would forget things when he was busy at work! Her tutor made her feel that a housewife and mother was a multi-talented, resourceful individual, and it was a mortal sin to say that one was 'just' a housewife. And this philosophy had an effect on Helen. She wondered whether she might not be capable of doing a fairly demanding job. As yet, she had no idea what she wanted to do, but she felt liberated from the home at last. Next year Katy would be starting school, and the opportunity was there. She was beginning to feel ambitious.

These days she had more energy. Her eating had become erratic. When she was working on an essay she would grab anything, eat too many mints. For the rest of the time, she simply joined in with the family – omelettes, chops, whatever. After leaving Slim-Plicity she had put on four or five pounds, but then she seemed to level out. Really she did not care about it any more. She was grateful to Slim-Plicity; through it she had met Sandra, and she had to admit that her weight loss did give her a feeling of achievement; a precursor, in fact, to what she was doing now. And yet she recognized that dieting was for her only a game. She could imagine a board game based on it, she could see it now: eat one packet of biscuits, go back three spaces; stay the same at the weekly weigh-in, miss a throw. (Too much snakes and ladders with the kids, she thought.) Perhaps she could market the game! The oddest thing was what had happened to Stella. Sandra had told her . . .

'What do I think about Anna's dancing? Well, I certainly never danced around the bedroom when I was six months' pregnant! I think Lawrence only sees what pregnancy represents, not what it actually feels like.'

'But didn't you feel full of joy when you were pregnant?'

'All I remember was the heartburn.'

The class laughed. The discussion continued, absorbing Helen completely. Outside, in the courtyard, the sunlight danced among the blackened stones. The sky was blue.

The turkey was browning nicely. Maureen spooned some more juice over it, and over the roasting potatoes, which would need a bit more cooking after the bird was done. It all smelled very appetizing. She closed the oven door and straightened up, rubbing her back as she did so. Time for a cup of tea. And some biscuits. There were some bourbons in the tin, she remembered. How wonderful not to be dieting! And of course, it was so lucky that she was not dieting at the moment, because they all had something to celebrate. That was why it was turkey this Sunday and not roast beef. Maureen was looking forward to making the trifle too. No one was around, and so she would allow herself the luxury of licking out the bowl. Her mouth watered.

Joe, Phil, Chris and Lisa were down at the Wellington, having a quick one before lunch. Sharon was round with Angie and the kids, and they said they'd arrive about one, to give Maureen a hand with laying out the table. Ought she to wait until they came round before she opened the sherry? The kitchen clock informed her it was just past midday. There was no reason why she shouldn't have a small one now; after all, it was a special occasion.

Three nights ago, Chris and Lisa had announced their engagement. At last! Maureen had wondered whether Lisa might be . . . But no! They had assured her it was simply because they had decided they were right for each other. They would get married just before Christmas, in Maureen's own church. The best thing about having a family was all these celebrations. The sherry was sweet and warming. But something was lacking. Peanuts! She opened the pantry and took out an economy-size packet of KP nuts, and poured a generous quantity into a glass bowl. It's strange how you grow to like some people. In the beginning she had thought Lisa was a bit too tough, an independent little madam. She was sure it was Lisa who had the idea of her son living in sin. But then Maureen remembered the time Lisa had brought round that cake and chocolate for her when she was at a low ebb one Sunday. True, she was supposed to be dieting. Or was it quite like that? Maureen frowned, and absently took some more nuts. Time to prepare the trifle.

They'd also arranged to go out to eat next weekend; Angie had said it was more of a treat if they could leave the kids with a baby-sitter. They'd go to the

Berni, probably, and that was bound to be a nice meal. In fact they had been there two weeks ago, just her and Joe. In her mind Maureen paraded all the 'posh' meals she had known. That Slim-Plicity buffet had been a disappointment, though. Everything was bite-size, insubstantial. She grimaced with distaste and the jelly dissolved. Mind you, she remembered Joe's face when she came home with bags full of leftovers. The pâté balls were a bit soggy but not too bad. They had finished them off with some cans of beer.

Slim-Plicity. It was good to give it a rest. Somebody told her that Stella had left. Maureen couldn't imagine Slim-Plicity without Stella. A shame, as she knew that she'd have to go back. Now there was the wedding at Christmas she would have to look good for the photographs. But she needn't think about it yet, not until after the summer holidays. That gave her (she calculated rapidly) one, two, three, four, five, six months. With an expert hand she stirred the custard. Six months of freedom. Mind you, it was fun at Slim-Plicity. She remembered the time when Stella had told them all never to go shopping when they were hungry, and Elsie (Maureen always thought she was a bit simple) had stuffed herself with two rounds of cheese sandwiches before every shopping expedition for that whole week. She'd put on two pounds and couldn't understand why! Yes, it was good to feel you belonged to Slim-Plicity. And even better when you didn't. Maureen sighed happily, running her finger round the custard-lined milk pan. Delicious!

'Well, it's quite nice.'

Sandra ate her lentil casserole without tremendous enthusiasm. It had been Cathy's idea to come to Beano's new eating place which had recently opened up on a site near the campus. Sandra had been to places like it before. The elderly formica tables wobbled slightly when you put pressure on them. Around the walls of the café were numerous posters informing the vegetarian clientele of matters of interest to them. Friends of the Earth advertised here; Sandra saw the familiar Greenpeace poster; what was rebirthing, she wondered? Fascinated, she read the poster next to it, which claimed that it was possible to achieve immortality here on earth, and all you had to do was believe that you were immortal. Cathy interrupted her perusal.

'Are you going to try the date and almond cake afterwards? Or are you still on that diet?'

'No, I'm not dieting, but I'm not really hungry.'

That sounded good, Sandra thought. She continued.

'I received my conditional acceptance from Huddersfield today.'

'Lovely. What is it you're doing? Teacher training? It's very high minded of you, taking charge of a class of bawling infants.'

'No, not infants, Cathy. I'm actually doing a PGCE in Adult Education. So I'll be training to teach in a college of further education, or a sixth form college. It won't be children; I might even end up teaching mature students.'

'Oh, I didn't realize. Does it pay better?'

'No, it's more or less the same. But it interests me,

giving people a second chance. I'm not absolutely sure I want to work with children.'

'I know what you mean. That's why I decided against educational psychology. I'm hoping to get in to do a diploma in personnel work. That's where the money is.'

'I'm surprised to hear you talk about money. You used to tell me that the only thing worth striving for was personal fulfilment.'

'Yes, well, I've discovered that for me, money equals personal fulfilment.'

Cathy moved some rather tough, inedible carrots around her plate with her fork.

'And so your personal fulfilment will be teaching adults. What about your ambitions to be slim?'

Sandra quickly turned on her. 'Why? Do you think I'm fat?'

'No.'

Sandra had to remind herself that she was supposed not to care whether she was fat or not. 'I am happy with the weight I am now,' she repeated to herself internally, 'I am happy with the weight I am now.' Emma had suggested to her that repeating certain phrases – affirmations, she called them – throughout the day would help her come to terms with her own body size. Sometimes she really felt it was working. Yet it took just one careless comment from Cathy to make the whole fragile edifice come tumbling down. I am happy with the weight I am now. I am happy with the weight I am now. It was funny how you could go off some people. She found she had less and less in common with Cathy these days. If only Emma lived nearer. But if I take up my place at Huddersfield, thought Sandra, I'll be quite near them. She watched Cathy return to the counter for some date and almond cake, and their coffees.

It was true; she wasn't dieting. It did not seem quite so important at the moment. It had been very absorbing, trying to find the right course, and she was certain now that Huddersfield Poly was right for her. It was interesting that her father had been very keen on her choice of career. Apparently his real worry was that she would end up doing nothing at all, and teaching seemed to him to be a proper job. He didn't even mind about supporting her another year. She was lucky in her parents. That realization, and her new sense of worth deriving from her firm choice of career, defused her anxiety about her weight. And yet . . .

She watched Cathy eat her cake, and she regretted slightly that she had not opted for some. Perhaps she would buy some in the wholefood shop next door. She could have a word with Martha too, if she was on the rota that day. If only she could lose her consciousness of food and its dangers. She watched Cathy with envy; imagine not caring at all about what you ate, and yet remaining slim. She'd put half a stone on over the Christmas vac, and lost two pounds of it in January. She hadn't weighed herself for at least a week, and that was a kind of victory, she supposed. Perhaps she wouldn't buy the cake next door. Or should she?

'Do you still see that friend of yours from the slimming club?'

'Who? Helen?'

'Mmm, yes. Her.'

'Oh, yes. I baby-sit for her. Or sometimes her husband baby-sits and we go out together. She's a good friend.'

'Has she put her weight back on?'

'We don't talk about weight any more,' said Sandra, untruthfully, as she often spoke to Helen about it, although Helen seemed not to need to do the same. And just now, Helen seemed to be much more of a friend than Cathy, whose comments seemed designed to disturb her equilibrium. I am happy with the weight I am now. Perhaps I ought to take up aerobics. That might burn some of it up. I am happy with the weight I am now.

They rose to leave the café. Sandra explained that she needed some provisions from the shop next door, but Cathy had a lecture, and so had to go. Sandra was relieved. And sure enough, there was Martha manning the tills. Or womanning the tills?

'Hi, Martha!'

'Sandra. Good to see you. You missed our last meeting.'

'I know. Essay crisis. And I can't get behind now. I really must start revising for finals soon. Only three months to go. Have you any date and almond cake left?'

'No. But try this carrot and banana cake. I think it's better. You will be at the national conference, won't you?'

Martha spoke sternly. Sandra smiled.

'Of course. I've offered to run the crèche. And I've promised to run a seminar on "The Fat Woman in Literature".'

'I might come to that.'

'Do. You'll enjoy it. Is Liz busy?'

'Yes. She's had a lot to do. I've been heavily involved in the women's refuge this month, and Liz has done most of the work for the conference. If it wasn't for Stella she'd be beside herself. But one thing I will say for Stella; she is organized, even if she does have quite a way to go.'

From Martha that was praise. Sandra grinned. Whenever she thought of the new Stella, she was filled with a strange kind of joy. Who would have imagined it? Next to her a bearded bespectacled student placed a wire basket full of packets of pulses in recycled polythene on to the counter. Sandra stood aside. Yes. She'd have some carrot and banana cake, and perhaps some wholemeal pizza for tea. Next week she'd watch what she ate more carefully. Perhaps!

Judith stepped gingerly on to the scales.

'Good! You've put on two pounds. How many weeks are you now? Sixteen? That's lovely. Right. If you could just sit down by the table I can take your blood pressure. There shouldn't be any problems at this stage.'

Around Judith's arm the nurse tied what looked like a thick black armband, and inflated it with air. Judith felt the pressure of it and tensed. She could not see the instrument the nurse was checking and hoped vaguely that she would be all right. She was.

Now for the embarrassing bit. Judith opened her handbag, unzipped a compartment at the side, and brought out a small jar of Colman's mustard, no longer

265

full of Colman's mustard, but containing her 'sample'. For her this was an ordeal. But the nurse, as she turned to the sink, hummed a tune and seemed perfectly at ease. I wouldn't fancy doing that all day long, thought Judith.

'Fine, love. Now if you could just get changed behind the screen we'll have you on the table for a quick look at that tummy.'

Judith did as she was asked and, behind the prettily patterned screen, stepped out of her grey skirt, folding it carefully and laying it over a chair. She was never quite at her ease in the doctor's surgery. This was perhaps because she was never sure what they were going to do with her. This was only her second visit to the doctor's about her pregnancy; three weeks ago she had been to the hospital. That was awful. She spent nearly all afternoon waiting for the series of tests – it was like an assembly line. And she wasn't allowed to go to the loo because the nurse told her that her bladder had to be full for the scan. She remembered twisting and turning on the hard seat. Then they covered her tummy with jelly and rolled something over it.

But that wasn't the worst of it. She remembered the interview with the registrar.

'Right, Mrs Pearce, what does your husband do?'

'He's a mini-cab driver but it's not his.'

'Sorry?'

'The baby's not his. I'm living with someone else. It's his.'

Her cheeks were on fire. Until this moment everything she had done with Geoff had seemed right and natural. Geoff coming to live with her seemed so right.

She stopped taking the pill then. She forgot to mention it to him. She enjoyed the gossip at work. She relished her next-door neighbour's curiosity and amused herself by telling the whole affair only piecemeal. Even during Christmas with the family she felt delightfully wicked.

But now, confronting stern-faced authority, she felt dirty. Suddenly she saw herself as a social inadequate. What would this woman think of her? Judith spoke again.

'We're getting married as soon as possible, that is, when the divorces come through.'

She'd tell that to Geoff tonight. She was sure he would agree to marriage. They'd spoken of it vaguely, and Len was bound to be happy with a divorce. Then she would be Mrs Hirst, and the baby would be Trevor Hirst, Trevor Frederick Hirst, after her grandfather, and he would have curly, sandy-coloured hair and look just like his daddy.

She lay supine on the examination table. The nurse felt her stomach with a firm pressure. It did not hurt. Judith was glad that as yet she did not seem appreciably fatter. That two pounds was a blow. She was trying to put on as little as possible. The books said that twenty pounds was a sufficient weight gain and she was determined to keep it at that. That was the worst part about being pregnant. After all those months spent losing it, you have to put it all back on again. Who would choose to be a woman! And what if she got stretch marks? Judith froze in horror. Would Geoff still fancy her with stretch marks? Well, she would just have to turn the lights off.

The nurse pressed a conical instrument against her tummy to listen for the baby's heartbeat. She was happy with Geoff. They went out a lot, and when they stayed in they hired videos. There was always something to do. Their sex life was good too. And Geoff believed there was a chance for promotion at the office. If this worked out, it would make things so much easier when the baby came along.

She rarely thought of Len. Once he had called in with Emma to collect something. They seemed very happy. She was so fat. Apparently they had left Oldham, and were living in Hebden Bridge, of all places. In one of those poky weaver's cottages, no doubt. Probably without central heating. Well, she had all that fat to keep her warm! She smiled to herself at her little joke. They were both working over there, he'd said. She was pleased they were at a distance.

'Everything seems to be fine, Mrs . . . er . . . Judith,' said the nurse, quickly glancing down at the notes in front of her. 'We won't need to see you for another month. Make your next appointment at reception. Is there anything you'd like to ask before you go?'

'No, thank you.'

Perhaps Trevor Frederick Geoffrey Hirst.

'*Your son, Mrs Hirst. What a handsome baby. May we take a photograph of him for the hospital records? Would you like us to call your husband in now? He has been so anxious for you.*' She freshened her make-up, took the baby in her arms and Geoff entered. '*My son!*'

She placed her hands on her hips, bent slowly down, and in slow motion, rotated her waist around in a circle. Empty your mind, she commanded herself, empty your mind.

But that was the part of yoga Stella found most difficult. Her mind kept filling with all manner of things. But then there was so much to think about these days! There was all the correspondence from the national conference, for one. And all the time she was making discoveries, discoveries about the oppression of women, discoveries about herself. Liz said she could only attend the conference as a guest speaker on the evils of slimming clubs, and not as a bona fide fat woman, as she was still quite slim.

She stood on one leg. She was disappointed to be excluded. She felt she had a lot to learn. It was import-ant for her to explore her relationship to fat, very important. And yet she couldn't see herself putting weight on simply for the conference. It was hard for her, eating without guilt. Part of her wanted to be fat, to be like Liz, Emma and the others. But no, it was impossible. She carried around in her head the calorie values of every known food, still restricted herself delib-erately. Even now, when she had joined the Fat Women's Support Group.

Stella did miss Slim-Plicity. But Liz had taught her that she missed the sense of importance it gave her, and she could learn to live without that. Stella had thought that she enjoyed helping people too. Maybe, said Liz, but you were misguided. Liz had taught her a lot. Stella was a real feminist now. Her mother was shocked. 'What! You mean you burn your bras? We'd be out of business!' It was good to shock her mother. That was one of the best things about being a feminist. And Richard was very kind about it all. He let her go to all the meetings she wanted.

She sat on the floor for some back stretches. Yes, feminism was very interesting. She'd never realized how oppressed she was. And then Emma had given her *Fat is a Feminist Issue* to read. She liked the title. The book fascinated her. Apparently all she had to do was eat whatever she liked when she was hungry and her weight would remain stable. But as she had told Emma, she didn't know what she liked any more. How could you like chocolate if it made you fat? Emma had to remind her that she didn't mind about being fat any more. Oh, yes!

And yet, out of all that confusion, something wonderful had grown. Something so wonderful that Stella even rationed her thoughts on the subject. She rolled over to attempt the cobra. Good! She had lifted herself higher than ever. But she must remember not to see yoga as a competition. It was that sense of competition, she had been told, that was her enemy.

She lay on her back, taking deep breaths. She tried to imagine that around her was the life-force, golden translucent air, and she was breathing it all in. And out. In. And out. Out with the tension, the competitiveness. In. Out.

And unbidden into her mind came Gill. Emma had told Stella that reading *Fat is a Feminist Issue* was not going to be enough for her. She needed real help. Emma had taken her one day to Gill Goldstein. Gill was a therapist. She used Gestalt, TA; she listened to Stella. She was American, from New York.

She was absolutely wonderful. Stella felt tremendous affection for Liz and Emma, but it was nothing to what she felt for Gill. She trusted Gill absolutely. She treasured everything she said. She breathed in deeply. Gill was taking her back through her childhood. And she was due for a therapy session that very evening. She smiled contentedly to herself. She worshipped no one as she worshipped Gill. At last she had found someone to look up to, someone to care for her, someone she could be like.

She breathed in Gill Goldstein. She breathed out Slim-Plicity. She would not allow herself to think about it, or him. She breathed in Gill. She breathed out her anxieties. Her stomach rose and fell. She breathed in the future, she breathed out the past.

In. Out.

SIGNET

Published or forthcoming

HAVING IT ALL

Maeve Haran

Having it All. Power. Money. Success. *And* a happy family. Liz really believed she could have it all. So when she's offered one of the most important jobs in television, she jumps at it.

But Liz discovers that there's a price to be paid for her success and that the whole glittering image is just an illusion. And one day she's faced with the choice she thought she'd never have to make.

Liz decides she *will* have it all – but on her own terms.

'Will touch cords, tug heartstrings. Every woman's been here' – Penny Vincenzi, author of *Old Sins*

'Realistic, compassionate, but still as pacey as they come' – *Cosmopolitan*

SIGNET

Published or forthcoming

The Stars Burn On

Denise Robertson

On New Year's Day 1980, Jenny and seven friends watch the dawn from a northern hill. On the brink of adulthood, confident of their futures, they vow to meet there again at the end of the decade. Just two weeks later, one of the group is dead. The others, irrevocably affected, go on to pursue careers in the law or media, and make new lives for themselves as husbands, wives and parents. Jenny, who establishes herself as a successful journalist in London, remains their lynchpin – and only Jenny knows that the secret that binds them is a lie.

'A saga that'll keep you turning the pages ... told with perception and humour' – *Prima*

'Her prose has a fine flow, her knowledge of the region is deep and instinctive. Above all, her compassion and great understanding of life show in all she writes' – *Evening Chronicle, Newcastle on Tyne*

Published or forthcoming

SIGNET

BASIC INSTINCT

Richard Osborne

A brutal murder.

A brilliant killer.

A cop who can't resist the danger.

When San Francisco detective Nick Curran begins investigating the mysterious and vicious murder of a rock star, he finds himself in a shadowy world where deceit and seduction often go hand in hand. Nick can't stay away from his number one suspect – stunning and uninhibited Catherine Tramell – a novelist whose shocking fiction mirrors the murder down to the smallest, bloodiest detail.

Entangled in love and murder, Nick is headed for trouble, with only his basic instinct for survival to keep him from making a fatal mistake…

SIGNET

Published or forthcoming

Lilies of the Field

Maureen O'Donoghue

Invited back to Trewythian, her long-lost island home, Sally leaves the sophisticated charm of London for the golden memories of her childhood.

As she is drawn into the warm embrace of the villagers, and intoxicated by a new romance, Sally's homecoming promises to be a joyous occasion. But the idyll turns sour when she stumbles upon a shocking secret from her family's past − a secret shared by a murderous assailant who stalks the island determined that she will never leave Trewythian again.

Unfolding against the sweeping moors and boundless skies of a gaunt and beautiful island, *Lilies of the Field* is a stirring, sensual tale of romance and adventure.

SIGNET

Published or forthcoming

THE GLITTERING STRAND

Judith Lennox

The Levant trade of the 1590's offers wealth and danger in equal measure. And, always, dreams ...

A dream for Serafina Guardi, captured by corsairs and sold into slavery *en route* to her profitable betrothal, struggling with the intrigues of the Italian cloth trade to reclaim her heritage – and revenge herself. And for Thomas Marlowe, the English pilot wrecked on the Barbary Coast, dreams of a ship such as the Mediterranean has never seen and wider seas to sail her in.

Chance and treachery conspire against their hopes while irretrievably entangling their fates. There will be long, hard years before either Serafina or Thomas comes near to their dream – only to find the dream is no longer the same...

Published or forthcoming

Blood Knot

Sam Llewellyn

Bill Tyrrell has locked the door on his crusading past. As a reporter, he's seen conflict and pain close up – and not once have his words ever saved a life. Now he's back in England, living on the antique cutter *Vixen*, the only legacy from his long-vanished father. But the journalist in him can't be buried. Not when a Russian sea cadet gets wrapped round the *Vixen's* propeller under the eyes of a Cabinet Minister – and Tyrrell becomes the scapegoat...

It is the first in a series of harrowing accidents. And suddenly the past begins to open up all over again, as Tyrrell's battle-hardened reporting reflexes lure him into a dark maze of political cover-ups and violent death...

'The best seabourne thriller in many a tide'
– *Daily Mail*

THE RATING GAME

Dave Cash

Behind the glass-fronted walls of CRFM's 24-hours-a-day nerve centre in the heart of London, three people fight for control of their lives as the tycoon powerbrokers of international finance move in for the kill...

Monica Hammond, the radio station's beautiful and ruthless Managing Director – nothing was allowed to stand in her way ... until one man discovered her fatal weakness.

Nigel Beresford-Clarke – CRFM's greatest asset – hopelessly betrayed by his love for a schoolgirl...

And **Maggie Lomax**, uncompromising and tough as nails – then her outspoken broadcasts pushed the wrong people too far ...

They're ready to play ... *The Rating Game*

SIGNET

Published or forthcoming

Ira Levin
author of *Rosemary's Baby*

Thirteen hundred Madison Avenue, an elegant 'sliver' building, soars high and narrow over Manhattan's smart Upper East Side. Kay Norris, a successful single woman, moves on to the twentieth floor of the building, high on hopes of a fresh start and the glorious Indian summer outside. But she doesn't know that someone is listening to her. Someone is *watching* her.

'Levin really knows how to touch the nerve ends' – *Evening Standard*

'*Sliver* is the ultimate *fin de siècle* horror novel, a fiendish goodbye-wave to trendy urban living ... Ira Levin has created the apartment dweller's worst nightmare' – Stephen King

Published or forthcoming

Liscombe Hall

Anne Griffiths

When an illicit liaison with Lord Liscombe ends in heartbreak, Kate Tranter sets out in search of a new life. Driven to protect a secret borne of passion, she rises beyond her humble beginnings to become a wealthy restaurateur; indomitable, proud, admired – and haunted by the searing memory of a love that could never be.

Set amidst the rolling hills of the Dorset countryside, from the turn of the century to the post-war era, *Liscombe Hall* follows the tangled destinies of two families and the powerful passions that bind them.

SIGNET

Published or forthcoming

TRIAL

Clifford Irving

They called it suppression of evidence and disbarred him from the 299th District Court for two long years.

Criminal Defence lawyer Warren Blackburn came back from the wilderness to pick up the crumbs – and found two cases just like the one that brought him down.

But this time he was ready to back his judgement and fight. Fight for justice and a fair trial against a legal system that would do anything as long as it got a deal...

'Riveting legal edge-of-the seater ... Has Texas and American Justice systems by the tail' – *Daily Telegraph*